GREEN MOUNTAIN

PELLET GRILL & SMOKER

COOKBOOK

FRESH AND FOOLPROOF RECIPES FOR YOUR GREEN MOUNTAIN PELLET GRILL & SMOKER

PETER RUBY

CONTENTS

INTRODUCTION

What Exactly Are Wood Pellets?

Wood pellets are made from a combination of hardwood shavings and sawdust. This is pressurized, compressed down, and held together through the use of the wood's lignin, an all-natural binding agent. It's made into long, pencil-thick rods that are broken into smaller pieces. Most wood pellet pieces will be about a half-inch long.

During the compression of the wood shaving and sawdust mixture, most of the air and moisture is removed. Also, this mixture means you won't be burning any bark, dirt, etc that you would find on raw wood logs. This results in an extremely efficient and clean-burning fuel source. Pellets used for smoking are also food-grade. Therefore, they do not contain any adhesives or chemicals. They also don't contain softwoods, like pine or spruce, that have a high amount of sap that can adversely affect the taste of your meat.

Most wood pellets are made up of mainly oak, a very stable burning wood. This is then blended with another hardwood or fruitwood to impart the flavor through the smoke.

The Operation Principle of Green Mountain Wood Pellet Grill

Wood pellet grills use an auger that moves the hardwood pellets from the hopper to the fire pot underneath the grill. The higher the set temperature, the more pellets are dispensed into the auger. Once in the fire pot, a hot rod ignites the pellets creating a fire, then a fan stokes the fire creating convection heat to evenly cook your food in the grill. A drip tray sits over the fire pot, keeping the direct flames off your food while catching food drippings to help prevent flare-ups.

The Advantages of Your Green Mountain Wood Pellet Grill

1. The Green Mountain wood pellet grill makes barbecuing easy.

Plug it in, fill the hopper with BBQ pellets, turn it on, set the temperature, and let the grill do the rest. Pellet grills are designed to allow one to take a hands-off approach to cooking by letting a controller do the majority of the work.

You don't need to haul logs or arrange charcoal. You can put away the lighter fluid and flint. The Ignition sequence on a pellet grill starts with a single button press.

Once the ignition sequence is complete, the controller's capabilities determine to what extent it is able to control the cooking process. Pellet grill controllers have evolved over time from simple low, medium, & high setting devices to the advanced controllers found on high end pellet grills today.

The programs and algorithms that comprise its firmware were designed by us to ensure peak performance, consistency, and accuracy whether you're grilling steaks in the sub-zero Alaskan winter or smoking a brisket all day in the blistering deserts of Arizona.

This level of control also allows you to choose cook length, temperature, and when that temperature should change. You're in control and can fully customize the longest and most complicated of cooks to your exact specifications.

Add to this the convenience of technologies like Wi-Fi and BlueTooth and it's easy to see the appeal of the work smarter, not harder approach to smoking and grilling meat.

2. The Green Mountain wood pellet grill is safe.

Gas can explode. Charcoal and wood logs are messy and can smolder for days after use. Direct cooking over fire increases the likelihood of flare ups and grease fires.

Pellet grills cook indirectly, meaning no open flame, flying sparks, or direct contact between fat drippings and fire. MAK Pellet grills create small, precisely controlled fires in a stainless-steel firepot. This firepot is surrounded by a stainless-steel body and covered by a stainless-steel diffuser, and drip pan at a minimum.

Pellets are released in small quantities and consumed completely. As long as you maintain relatively minimal cleaning routines, which we make as easy as possible by using a removable firepot, the chances of anything out of the ordinary happening are extremely low.

The pellet grill is the safest outdoor cooking device ever invented.

3.Pellet grilling is better for your health and the environment. No added oils or fats are needed to achieve the tremendous flavor that cooking on a pellet grill imparts. You're cooking with real wood, which means you're using a fuel that has been used since the dawn of time. Because you are cooking indirectly, excess animal fat drippings are not burned up and made carcinogenic by open flame. Instead, they hit a grease pan and convert to gases which help flavor your food. Hardwood BBQ pellets burn with a more than 98% efficiency. This reduces the exposure of carcinogenic substances and HCA's to you and the environment. Avoiding the creation of carcinogenic smoke is not only good for your health. Extremely low particulate matter means fresher, safer air to breathe. Barbecue pellets reduce landfill disposal of sawdust by millions of tons per year. Barbecue pellets are not only a sustainable biofuel, they are also the ultimate example of re-purposing.

Tips for Using Your Green Mountain Wood Pellet Grill

1. Season your new pellet grill.
Season your new pellet grill according to the manufacturer's directions (a process that usually takes 45 minutes to one hour). This burns off any residual oils from the manufacturing process.

2. Allow yourself some time to get acquainted with your new grill/smoker.
Allow yourself some time to get acquainted with your new grill/smoker. We know you'll be anxious to try it out, but don't be overly ambitious. Instead of a whole brisket, which could take 15 hours or more, or a budget-busting prime rib roast, start with chicken (parts, such as breasts or wings, or a whole bird), pork loin tenderloin, or blade (shoulder) steaks, Cornish hens, salmon steaks or fillets, or other relatively inexpensive cuts that can be completed in 2 hours or less.

3. Identify any hot spots—most grills have them.
Identify any hot spots—most grills have them. Preheat your grill to medium-high as directed by the owner's manual, then lay slices of cheap white bread shoulder to shoulder across the grate. Watch carefully, then flip after a few minutes. Take a photo of the results. The darkest bread will indicate where the temperature might be hotter. (Print the photo out and add it to your owner's manual for reference.)

4. Don't let your meat come to room temperature before cooking.

Whatever meat you select, put it on the preheated grill/smoker straight from the refrigerator. Do not, as many recipes suggest, allow it to come to room temperature before cooking.

As Steven often notes, high-end steak houses do not leave their meats out at room temperature. (The danger area is 40 to 140 degrees.) The heat of the grill is sufficient to raise the internal temperature of the meat by those few degrees.

5. Invest in a good meat thermometer.

A laser-type thermometer such as this one will give you a more accurate temperature reading at grill level than a built-in dome thermometer. Determine the temperature range of your grill model from lowest to highest (180 degrees to 500+, for example).

Cleaning Your Green Mountain Wood Pellet Grill

For spot-cleaning the outside of your grill, you can simply use a dry cloth to remove grease marks, dust and dirt quickly. To perform a deep clean, use a soft cloth with soap and water, stainless steel cleaner or a bbq degreaser. Follow these steps to clean the outside of your BBQ:

1. Make sure your grill is cold before spraying any cleaner on the outside of your grill.
2. Apply your cleaner using a soft cloth or spray bottle. If spraying cleaner onto your pellet grill, be very careful not to get any inside of your grill. Avoid spraying stainless steel cleaner onto plastic components as it can cause them to degrade more quickly.
3. Allow the cleaner to sit for at least 30 seconds to break down any dried grease or food residue.
4. Wipe the cleaner off with a clean cloth or paper towel. If cleaning a stainless steel BBQ, wipe in the same direction as the grain. If your smoker has a painted surface, wipe in circles.
5. Repeat this process as necessary until all of the dirt and grime is removed.
6. Using a wet cloth, wipe down the surface of the grill to remove all remaining cleaner or soap residue. Do not rinse your pellet grill with a hose or bucket as water can get into the grill or hopper and cause damage its electrical components or ruin the pellets.

Always unplug your pellet grill from its power source before cleaning it with water or liquid cleaner and allow it to dry for at least 24 hours before your next grilling session. Empty your wood pellets from the hopper before cleaning and check that there is no water or cleaner in the hopper before putting the pellets back in.

PORK RECIPES

St. Louis–style Pork Steaks

Servings: 4

Cooking Time: 120 Minutes

Ingredients:

- 1 cup low-carb barbecue sauce
- ¼ cup low-carb beer or sugar-free dark-colored soda or sugar-free root beer
- 4 bone-in pork shoulder steaks, each about 1lb (450g) and at least 1 inch (2.5cm) thick
- for the rub
- 1 tbsp coarse salt
- 1 tbsp freshly ground black pepper
- 1 tbsp granulated light brown sugar or low-carb substitute
- 1 tbsp sweet or smoked paprika
- 1 tsp granulated garlic or garlic powder
- 1 tsp celery salt

Directions:

1. Supply your smoker with wood pellets and follow the start-up procedure. Preheat the grill, with the lid closed, to 250° F.

2. In a small bowl, combine the barbecue sauce and beer. Set aside.

3. In a small bowl, make the rub by combining the ingredients. Mix well. Season the steaks on both sides with some of the rub.

4. Place the steaks on the grate at an angle to the bars and smoke for 30 minutes. Transfer the steaks to an aluminum foil roasting pan. Pour the barbecue mixture over them. Use tongs to turn the steaks, making sure each is coated well with the sauce.

5. Tightly wrap aluminum foil over the top of the pan and place it on the grate. Braise the steaks until they're fork tender, about 1½ hours. (Protect your hands when lifting a corner of the foil because steam will escape.)

6. Remove the pan from the grill and serve the steaks immediately.

Bacon Stuffed Onion Rings

Servings: 6

Cooking Time: 120 Minutes

Ingredients:

- ➢ 1 Pack Bacon
- ➢ 2 White Onions

Directions:

1. Supply your smoker with wood pellets and follow the start-up procedure. Preheat the grill, with the lid open, to 250° F.

2. Peel each onion and cut into thirds, separating the onion slices into rings. Using two slices of bacon, wrap around the onion ring until the ring is fully covered, securing in place with a toothpick. Continue until all the bacon is used up.

3. Place the onion rings on the and smoke until the bacon is cooked, about 120 minutes.

Grilled Lemon Pepper Pork Tenderloin

Servings: 4

Cooking Time: 20 Minutes

Ingredients:

- 2 lemons, zested
- 1 Clove garlic, minced
- 1 Teaspoon freshly minced parsley
- 1 Teaspoon lemon juice
- 1/4 Teaspoon black pepper
- 1/2 Teaspoon kosher salt
- 2 Tablespoon olive oil
- 1 (2 lb) pork tenderloin

Directions:

1. In a small bowl, whisk together everything except the tenderloin.
2. Trim all silverskin and excess fat from the tenderloin.
3. Place pork in a large resealable bag. Pour the marinade over the tenderloin and zip closed. Transfer to the refrigerator and marinate for at least 2 hours but no more than 8.
4. Supply your smoker with wood pellets and follow the start-up procedure. Preheat the grill, with the lid closed, to 375° F.
5. Remove the tenderloin from the bag and discard the marinade.
6. When the grill is hot, place tenderloin directly on the grill grate and cook 15 to 20 minutes, flipping once halfway through until the internal temperature reaches 145°F. Grill: 375 °F Probe: 145 °F
7. Remove from the heat and let rest 5 to 10 minutes before slicing. Enjoy!

Smoked Bologna

Servings: 4

Cooking Time: 240 Minutes

Ingredients:

- ➢ 1 Pound bologna log
- ➢ 1/4 Cup brown sugar
- ➢ 1 Tablespoon yellow mustard
- ➢ 1 Teaspoon soy sauce
- ➢ Worcestershire sauce

Directions:

1. Score the bologna log being careful not to cut too deep.
2. Mix brown sugar, mustard, soy sauce and Worcestershire sauce together.
3. Once mixed, rub it all over the bologna.
4. Supply your smoker with wood pellets and follow the start-up procedure. Preheat the grill, with the lid closed, to 225° F.
5. Smoke bologna for 3 to 4 hours. Grill: 225 ˚F
6. Remove from grill and let cool.
7. Slice and serve with sandwiches. Enjoy!

Bbq Pulled Pork With Sweet & Heat Bbq Sauce

Servings: 4

Cooking Time: 540 Minutes

Ingredients:

- 10 Pound Bone-In Pork Butt
- 2 Tablespoon Pork & Poultry Rub
- 1 1/2 Cup apple juice
- 4 Tablespoon brown sugar
- 1 Tablespoon salt
- 1 To Taste salt
- 1 To Taste Pork & Poultry Rub
- 1 As Needed Sweet & Heat BBQ Sauce

Directions:

1. Trim pork butt of all excess fat leaving 1/4" of the fat cap attached. Combine 2 Tbsp Pork and Poultry rub, apple juice, brown sugar, and salt in a small bowl stirring until most of the sugar and salt are dissolved. Inject the pork butt every square inch or so with the apple juice mixture. Season the exterior of the pork butt with remaining rub.

2. Supply your smoker with wood pellets and follow the start-up procedure. Preheat the grill, with the lid closed, to 225° F.

3. Place pork butt directly on the grill grate and cook for about 6 hours or until the internal temperature reaches 160°F. Grill: 225 °F Probe: 160 °F

4. Wrap the pork butt in two layers of foil and pour in 1/2 cup of apple juice. Secure tin foil tightly to contain the apple juice. Increase temperature to 275°F and return to grill in a pan large enough to hold the pork butt in case of leaks. Cook an additional 3 hours or until internal temperature reaches 205°F. Grill: 275 °F Probe: 205 °F

5. Remove from the grill and discard the bone. Shred the pork removing any excess fat or tendons. Season with additional Pork and Poultry Rub and salt if needed.

6. Add Sweet & Heat BBQ sauce and serve. Enjoy!

Smoked Ham

Servings: 12-15

Cooking Time: 300 Minutes

Ingredients:

- ➢ 1 (10-pound) fresh ham, skin removed
- ➢ 2 tablespoons olive oil
- ➢ 1 batch Rosemary-Garlic Lamb Seasoning

Directions:

1. Supply your smoker with wood pellets and follow the start-up procedure. Preheat the grill, with the lid closed, to 180°F.

2. Rub the ham all over with olive oil and sprinkle it with the seasoning.

3. Place the ham directly on the grill grate and smoke for 3 hours.

4. Increase the grill's temperature to 375°F and continue to smoke the ham until its internal temperature reaches 170°F.

5. Remove the ham from the grill and let it rest for 10 minutes, before carving and serving.

Cider Glazed Baked Holiday Ham

Servings: 6

Cooking Time: 120 Minutes

Ingredients:

- 3 apples, cored and cut into thick slices
- 1 Large ham
- 4 Cup apple cider, divided
- 1/4 Cup bourbon
- 1/4 Cup Dijon mustard
- 1/4 Cup honey or maple syrup
- 1/2 Teaspoon ground cinnamon
- 1/4 Teaspoon ground cloves
- 1 Pinch ground nutmeg or allspice

Directions:

1. Supply your smoker with wood pellets and follow the start-up procedure. Preheat the grill, with the lid closed, to 325° F.

2. Line a roasting pan with heavy-duty foil for easier clean-up.

3. Arrange the apple slices in the bottom of the roasting pan for a natural roasting rack. Place ham on top of the apple slices and pour remaining 1 cup of apple cider around the ham.

4. Place roasting pan directly on grill grate and bake for 1-1/2 hours. Grill: 325 °F

5. For the glaze, combine remaining 3 cups of apple cider and bourbon in a small saucepan and bring to a boil over medium-high heat. Simmer until reduced by one-third. Whisk in the mustard, honey, cinnamon, cloves and nutmeg.

6. Glaze ham with apple cider mixture as needed (use any left over for serving) and continue cooking for another 30 minutes or until a thermometer inserted into the thickest part of the meat reaches an internal temperatures of 140°F. Grill: 325 °F Probe: 140 °F

7. Remove ham from grill and allow to rest for 20 minutes before serving.

8. Warm remaining sauce and serve with ham if desired. Enjoy!

Smoked Rendezvous Ribs

Servings: 4

Cooking Time: 120 Minutes

Ingredients:

- 1/2 Cup apple cider vinegar
- 1/2 Cup water
- 1/2 Cup BBQ Sauce
- 2 Tablespoon Pork & Poultry Rub
- 3 Rack baby back pork ribs, membrane removed
- 1 As Needed Pork & Poultry Rub

Directions:

1. In a mixing bowl, combine vinegar, water, barbecue sauce, and Traeger Pork and Poultry rub. Set the sauce and a barbecue mop or basting brush grill-side.

2. Supply your smoker with wood pellets and follow the start-up procedure. Preheat the grill, with the lid closed, to 325° F.

3. Arrange the ribs on the grill grate, meat-side up.

4. Grill for 30 minutes, then start mopping. Mop every 15 minutes. After 2 hours, check the ribs for doneness. Grill: 325 °F

5. Insert a toothpick between the bones in the center of a rack. If there is little or no resistance, the ribs are done (or close to it). If the ribs are not to your liking, continue to grill them in 30-minute increments, mopping every 15 minutes. Grill: 325 °F

6. When the ribs are done, transfer them to a cutting board and give them a final dose of the mop sauce. Sprinkle lightly with Traeger Pork and Poultry Rub.

7. Let the ribs rest for a few minutes before cutting into half slabs or individual ribs. Enjoy!

Spiced Pork Belly

Servings: 4

Cooking Time: 130 Minutes

Ingredients:

- 2lb (1kg) skinless pork belly
- for the rub
- 2 tbsp fine kosher salt
- 2 tbsp granulated white or light brown sugar or low-carb substitute
- 2 tsp freshly ground black pepper
- 2 tsp ground mustard
- 2 tsp Chinese five-spice powder

Directions:

1. In a small bowl, make the rub by combining the ingredients. Mix well. Lightly season the pork belly on all sides with the rub. Cover and refrigerate overnight.

2. Supply your smoker with wood pellets and follow the start-up procedure. Preheat the grill, with the lid closed, to 450° F.

3. Place the pork belly on the grate and roast for 30 minutes, turning once. Lower the temperature to 275°F (135°C). Roast the pork until tender and the internal temperature reaches 185°F (85°C), about 1 to 1½ hours more.

4. Remove the pork belly from the grill and let cool completely. Wrap tightly in plastic wrap and refrigerate until firm and well chilled.

5. Preheat the grill to 450°F (232°C).

6. Cut the pork belly into slices, slabs, or cubes. Place the pork on the grate and grill until the edges crisp, about 8 to 10 minutes, turning as needed.

7. Remove the pork from the grill and serve immediately.

Pickle Brined Grilled Pork Chops

Servings: 4

Cooking Time: 60 Minutes

Ingredients:

- ➢ 4 pork chops
- ➢ 3 Cup Dill Pickle Brine, jar
- ➢ coarse ground black pepper, divided

Directions:

1. Put the pork chops and pickle brine in a resealable plastic bag. Refrigerate for at least 4 hours. Drain well and pat dry with paper towels.

2. Season generously with black pepper.

3. Supply your smoker with wood pellets and follow the start-up procedure. Preheat the grill, with the lid closed, to 300° F.

4. Put the chops directly on the grill grate and grill, turning once, for about 1 hour, or until the internal temperature of the chop is at least 145°F. Grill: 300 °F Probe: 145 °F

5. Let rest for 5 minutes before serving. Enjoy!

Old-fashioned Roasted Glazed Ham

Servings: 8

Cooking Time: 60 Minutes

Ingredients:

➤ 1 (10 lb) fully cooked bone-in spiral cut ham

➤ 1 Cup pineapple juice

➤ 1/2 Cup brown sugar

➤ 1 cinnamon stick

➤ 14 whole cloves

➤ 1 Whole Pineapple, fresh

➤ 10 Cherries, fresh, sweet

Directions:

1. Supply your smoker with wood pellets and follow the start-up procedure. Preheat the grill, with the lid closed, to 325° F.

2. Rinse ham under cold water and pat dry with paper towel.

3. In a saucepan combine pineapple juice, brown sugar, cinnamon stick and four cloves. Bring to a boil. Reduce heat to medium low and simmer for about 15 minutes or until pineapple juice is reduced by half, thick and syrupy.

4. Brush half of the glaze onto the ham and into the folds of the cut slices. Reserve the other half of the glaze for later.

5. Cut pineapple in desired sized pieces, about 2 inch squares, then place on ham with a cherry and a clove to pin in place, repeating all over ham.

6. Put ham in a deep baking dish with fat side up. Place on the Traeger and cook for about 1-¼ hours. Grill: 325 °F

7. Carefully remove from Traeger and brush remaining glaze onto ham.

8. Return ham to Traeger and continue cooking for another 15 to 20 minutes, until internal temperature of ham reaches 160°F. Grill: 325 °F Probe: 160 °F

9. Allow ham to rest for 15 – 20 minutes before serving. Enjoy!

Pulled Pork Corn Tortillas

Servings: 4

Cooking Time: 15 Minutes

Ingredients:

- Cilantro
- Cilantro, Chopped
- 8 Corn Tortillas
- Jalepeno, Sliced
- 1 Lime, Wedges
- 2 Cups Pulled Pork
- Radishes, Sliced
- White Onion, Diced

Directions:

1. Supply your smoker with wood pellets and follow the start-up procedure. Preheat the grill, with the lid open, to 350° F. Grill the corn tortillas until they are softened and have charred spots, about 30 seconds.

2. To assemble the carnitas, add the pulled pork to the tortillas, and top with radishes, diced onion, cilantro, jalapeno and a squeeze of lime juice, if desired. Serve and enjoy!

BAKING RECIPES

Baked Pumpkin Pie

Servings: 6

Cooking Time: 50 Minutes

Ingredients:

- 4 Ounce cream cheese
- 15 Ounce pumpkin puree
- 1/3 Cup Cream, whipping
- 1/2 Cup brown sugar
- 1 Teaspoon pumpkin pie spice
- 3 Large eggs
- 1 frozen pie crust, thawed

Directions:

1. Supply your smoker with wood pellets and follow the start-up procedure. Preheat the grill, with the lid closed, to 325° F.

2. Mix cream cheese, puree, milk, sugar, and spice. One at a time, incorporate an egg to the mixture. Pour mixture into pie shell.

3. Bake for 50 minutes, edges should be golden and pie should be firm around edges with slight movement in middle. Let cool before whip cream is applied. Serve and enjoy! Grill: 325 °F

Garlic Cheese Pull Apart Bread

Servings: 2

Cooking Time: 20 Minutes

Ingredients:

- ➢ 1 Loaf Bread, Sourdough Round
- ➢ 2 1/2 Tbsp Butter, Salted
- ➢ 8 Oz Fontina Cheese
- ➢ 1 Grated Garlic, Roasted
- ➢ 1/4 Cup Parsley, Minced Fresh
- ➢ 1 Tsp Red Flakes Pepper
- ➢ 1 Pinch Salt

Directions:

1. Start your Grill on "smoke" with the lid open until a fire is established in the burn pot (3-7 minutes). Supply your smoker with wood pellets and follow the start-up procedure. Preheat the grill, with the lid closed, to 300° F.

2. In a small bowl, add the soft butter, grated garlic, red pepper flakes, sea salt, and ¼ cup of the chopped parsley, and whisk together. With a bread serrated knife, cut 1-inch slices into the bread, not cutting all the way through the bottom of the load. With a butter knife, spread a thin layer of the butter mixture on each slice of the bread. Take the serrated knife again, and cut across the loaf to form 1 inch squares. Next, slice the cheese into small thin slices, then stuff one slice into each bread opening. Place the bread on a baking sheet, and cover tightly with aluminum foil. Place on the grill for about 10 minutes, remove the foil, and grill for a few more minutes until the top is nicely golden and the cheese is oozing. Remove from the grill, sprinkle with fresh parsley leaves, then serve.

Marbled Brownies With Amaretto & Ricotta

Servings: 4

Cooking Time: 30 Minutes

Ingredients:

- 1 Cup Ricotta Cheese
- 1 eggs
- 1 Tablespoon Amaretto Liqueur
- 1/4 Cup sugar
- 2 Teaspoon cornstarch
- 1/2 Teaspoon vanilla extract
- 1 Brownie Mix

Directions:

1. Coat a 9- by 13-inch nonstick baking pan with cooking spray or softened butter and set aside. (If you do not have a nonstick pan, line a regular one with buttered foil or parchment paper.)

2. In a medium bowl, combine the ricotta, egg, amaretto, sugar, cornstarch, and vanilla and whisk together thoroughly. Set aside.

3. Prepare the brownie mix according to the package directions. Spread the brownie batter evenly in the prepared pan. Randomly drop dollops of the ricotta mixture over the batter. Run a plastic knife through the ricotta mixture to give the brownies a marbled look. (A plastic knife is less likely to scratch your pan's nonstick surface.)

4. Supply your smoker with wood pellets and follow the start-up procedure. Preheat the grill, with the lid closed, to 350° F.

5. Put the pan with the brownie mixture directly on the grill grate and bake, about 25 to 30 minutes. Insert a bamboo skewer or toothpick in the center of the brownies to determine if they are done: the batter should not be wet. Grill: 350 °F

6. Transfer the brownies to a wire cooling rack to cool completely. Cut into squares.

Vanilla Chocolate Chip Cookies

Servings: 12

Cooking Time: 20 Minutes

Ingredients:

- ➢ 3/4 cup brown sugar
- ➢ 3/4 cup white sugar
- ➢ 1 stick butter, room temp
- ➢ 2 eggs
- ➢ 1 tsp vanilla
- ➢ 2 1/2 cups flour
- ➢ 1/2 tsp salt
- ➢ 1 tsp baking soda
- ➢ 1 cup Chocolate Chips

Directions:

1. Cream your butter and sugar together in a mixing bowl using a hand mixer or stand mixer on medium speed for about 4-5 minutes.

2. Once the butter is creamed, add the eggs and vanilla. Continue mixing for an additional minute.

3. Put flour, salt, and baking soda in a sifter. Sift it into your creamed butter mixture.

4. Scrape the sides of your mixing bowl with a rubber spatula, and then turn your mixer on to low speed.

5. Let it mix a little, and then scrape the sides again. Stop mixing when there are one or two streaks of flour left in the cookie dough.

6. Scrape the sides of your bowl and pour in a cup of chocolate chips, and turn the mixer to low again to mix the chocolate. It should take just a few turns for the chocolate pieces to be well incorporated.

7. Line a large baking sheet with parchment paper. Using a medium cookie scoop (about 1.5 tbsp), drop evenly spaced dollops of cookie dough onto the cookie sheet.

8. Supply your smoker with wood pellets and follow the start-up procedure. Preheat the grill, with the lid closed, to 350° F. Place the cookie sheet in your smoker, and let them cook for about 12 minutes.

9. Let them sit on a cooling rack while you continue to cook the additional cookies.

10. Cool for a few minutes to let cookies set.

11. Enjoy!

Anzac Coconut Biscuits

Servings: 4

Cooking Time: 30 Minutes

Ingredients:

- ➢ This recipe makes a dozen biscuits.
- ➢ 1 cup rolled oats
- ➢ 3/4 cup raw sugar
- ➢ 3/4 cup desiccated coconut
- ➢ 1 cup plain flour, sifted
- ➢ 125 g butter, melted
- ➢ 2 tablespoons Golden Syrup
- ➢ 1/2 tsp bicarb soda
- ➢ 3 tablespoons boiling water

Directions:

1. Combine and mix thoroughly sifted flour, oats, sugar and coconut in a large bowl.
2. Melt the butter and Golden Syrup over low heat.
3. Add boiling water to the bicarb soda, once dissolved add into the butter/syrup mix, it will bubble/fizz up a bit.
4. Add the liquid into the dry ingredients and mix throughly.
5. Rolls the mix into golf ball size balls and layout on grease proof paper on baking tray and flatten the tops just slightly.
6. Space the balls with about 3 fingers between each ball as they will flatten to about triple the diameter as they cook.
7. Supply your smoker with wood pellets and follow the start-up procedure. Preheat the grill, with the lid closed, to 350° F. Cook for 25-30 minutes until golden brown.
8. Rest on cooling rack until at room temperature then store in air-tight container.

Smoked, Salted Caramel Apple Pie

Servings: 4

Cooking Time: 60 Minutes

Ingredients:

- 1 Cup cream
- 1 Cup brown sugar
- 3/4 Cup Light Corn Syrup
- 6 Tablespoon butter
- 1 Teaspoon sea salt
- 1 Pastry for Double-Crust Pie
- 6 Granny Smith Apples, Cut Into Wedges

Directions:

1. Supply your smoker with wood pellets and follow the start-up procedure. Preheat the grill, with the lid closed, to 180° F.

2. Fill a large pan with ice and water. Pour the cream into a smaller, shallow pan. Place the pan with the cream in the ice bath and place them both on the Traeger to smoke for 15-20 minutes. Grill: 180 °F

3. To make the caramel, combine the sugar and corn syrup in a saucepan and cook over medium heat, stirring constantly until it coats the back of your spoon and starts to turn a copper color, then stir in butter, salt, and smoked cream.

4. To assemble the pie, gather the pie crust, salted caramel, and apples. Place one of the pie crusts into the pie plate and fill with apple slices. Pour caramel over the apples. Lay the top crust over the filling, then crimp the top and bottom crusts together.

5. Make slits in the top crust to release the steam and finish by brushing with egg or cream. Sprinkle with raw sugar and sea salt.

6. When ready to bake, set the Traeger to 375°F and preheat, lid closed for 15 minutes.

7. Place the pie on the grill and bake for 20 minutes. Grill: 375 °F

8. Reduce heat to 325°F and cook for 25 more minutes. When ready, the crust should be golden brown and the filling, bubbly. Grill: 325 °F

9. Remove the pie from the grill and let cool. Serve with vanilla ice cream. Enjoy!

Delicious Smoked Candied Pecan Pie

Servings: 4

Cooking Time: 55 Minutes

Ingredients:

- 1 cup brown sugar
- 1/4 cup granulated sugar
- 1 1/2 teaspoon vanilla
- 1/2 teaspoon corn starch
- 1/2 teaspoon orange zest
- 1/2 teaspoon salt
- 3/4 cup light corn syrup
- 1/2 cup butter (aka- 1 stick), melted
- 3 eggs, beaten
- 1 1/2 cups smoked candied pecans
- 1 pie crust

Directions:

1. Supply your smoker with wood pellets and follow the start-up procedure. Preheat the grill, with the lid closed, to 350° F.

2. Put brown sugar, granulated sugar, vanilla, corn starch, orange zest, salt, light corn syrup, melted butter, and three eggs in a medium mixing bowl. Stir ingredients together.

3. Lightly grease a pie pan and put your rolled out pie crust in. Make sure pie crust conforms to the pie tin. Sprinkle half of your pecans onto pie crust in pie pan. Pour ingredients from mixing bowl into pie pan, then evenly top with the remaining pecans.

4. Cover pie in foil and put on the grill. After 30 minutes, remove foil and cook for another 25 minutes.

5. Remove the pecan pie from grill and let it cool to room temperature before serving.

Zucchini Bread

| Servings: 6 | Cooking Time: 50 Minutes |

Ingredients:

- 1 Cup Walnuts, Chopped
- 2 Large zucchini
- 1 Teaspoon salt
- 1 Teaspoon ground cinnamon
- 1/4 Teaspoon ground cloves
- 1/4 Teaspoon baking powder
- 3 Cup all-purpose flour
- 1 eggs
- 2 Cup sugar
- 1/2 Cup vegetable oil
- 1/2 Cup Yogurt
- 1 1/2 Teaspoon vanilla extract

Directions:

1. Grease and flour two 9- by 5-inch bread pans, preferably nonstick.

2. When ready to cook, set the temperature to 350°F and preheat, lid closed for 15 minutes.

3. Spread the walnuts on a pie plate and toast for 10 minutes, stirring once. Let cool, then coarsely chop. Set aside.

4. Trim the ends off the zucchini, then coarsely grate into a colander set over the sink on a box grater (or use the shredding disk on a food processor). You'll need 2 cups.

5. Sprinkle with the salt and let drain for 30 minutes. Press on the zucchini with paper towels to expel excess water.

6. Sift the flour, baking powder, cinnamon, and cloves in a mixing bowl or on a large sheet of parchment or wax paper.

7. Combine the eggs, sugar, oil, yogurt, and vanilla in a large mixing bowl and mix on medium speed. (You can mix the batter by hand, if desired.) Add half the dry ingredients and mix on low speed; add the remaining dry ingredients and mix until just combined.

8. Stir in the walnuts and zucchini by hand.

9. Divide the batter between the prepared baking pans.

10. Arrange the pans directly on the grill grate and bake for 50 minutes, or until a bamboo skewer inserted in the center of the breads comes out clean.

11. Transfer to a wire rack and let cool for 10 minutes, then remove the breads from the pans. For best results, let the breads cool completely before slicing.

Baked Wood-fired Pizza

Servings: 6   Cooking Time: 12 Minutes

Ingredients:

- 2/3 Cup warm water (110°F to 115°F)
- 2 1/2 Teaspoon active dry yeast
- 1/2 Teaspoon granulated sugar
- 1 Teaspoon kosher salt
- 1 Tablespoon oil
- 2 Cup all-purpose flour
- 1/4 Cup fine cornmeal
- 1 Large grilled portobello mushroom, sliced
- 1 Jar pickled artichoke hearts, drained and chopped
- 1 Cup shredded fontina cheese
- 1/2 Cup shaved Parmigiano-Reggiano cheese, divided
- To Taste Roasted Garlic, minced
- 1/4 Cup extra-virgin olive oil
- To Taste banana peppers

Directions:

1. In a glass bowl, stir together the warm water, yeast and sugar. Let stand until the mixture starts to foam, about 10 minutes. In a mixer, combine 1-3/4 cup flour, sugar and salt. Stir oil into the yeast mixture. Slowly add the liquid to the dry ingredients while slowly increasing the mixers speed until fully combined. The dough should be smooth and not sticky.

2. Knead the dough on a floured surface, gradually adding the remaining flour as needed to prevent the dough from sticking, until smooth, about 5 to 10 minutes.

3. Form the dough into a ball. Apply a thin layer of olive oil to a large bowl. Place the dough into the bowl and coat the dough ball with a small amount of olive oil. Cover and let rise in a warm place for about 1 hour or until doubled in size.

4. When ready to cook, set smoker temperature to 450°F and preheat, lid closed for 15 minutes.

5. Place a pizza stone in the grill while it preheats.

6. Punch the dough down and roll it out into a 12-inch circle on a floured surface.

7. Spread the cornmeal evenly on the pizza peel. Place the dough on the pizza peel and assemble the toppings evenly in the following order: olive oil, roasted garlic, fontina, portobello, artichoke hearts, Parmigiano-Reggiano and banana peppers.

8. Carefully slide the assembled pizza from the pizza peel to the preheated pizza stone and bake until the crust is golden brown, about 10 to 12 minutes. Enjoy!

Pumpkin Bread

Servings: 6	Cooking Time: 60 Minutes

Ingredients:

- 1 Cup Pumpkin, canned
- 2 eggs
- 2/3 Cup vegetable oil
- 1/2 Cup sour cream
- 1 Teaspoon vanilla extract
- 2 1/2 Cup flour
- 1 1/2 Teaspoon baking soda
- 1 Teaspoon salt
- 1/2 Teaspoon ground cinnamon
- 1/4 Teaspoon ground nutmeg
- 1/4 Teaspoon ground cloves
- 1/4 Teaspoon ground ginger
- As Needed butter

Directions:

1. In a large mixing bowl, combine the pumpkin, eggs, vegetable oil, sour cream, and vanilla and whisk to blend.

2. In a separate bowl, combine the flour, baking soda, salt, cinnamon, nutmeg, cloves, and ginger. Add the dry ingredients to the wet ingredients and stir to combine. Do not overmix.

3. If desired, stir in one or more of the optional ingredients (walnuts, dried cranberries, raisins, or chocolate chips). Butter the interiors of two loaf pans.

4. Sprinkle with flour to coat the buttered surfaces, and tap out any excess. Divide the batter evenly between the two pans.

5. When ready to cook, set the smoker to 350°F and preheat, lid closed for 15 minutes.

6. Arrange the loaf pans directly on the grill grate. Bake for 45 to 50 minutes, or until a skewer or toothpick inserted in the center comes out clean. Also, the top of the loaf should spring back when pressed gently with a finger.

7. Transfer the loaf pans to a cooling rack and let cool for 10 minutes before carefully turning out the pumpkin bread. Let the loaves cool thoroughly before slicing. Wrap in aluminum foil or plastic wrap if not eating right away. Serve and enjoy!

Smoked Sweet Beer Bread

Servings: 6

Cooking Time: 60 Minutes

Ingredients:

- 3 cups all-purpose flour, sifted
- 2 tbsp. sugar
- 1 tbsp. baking powder
- 1 tsp. salt
- 1 (12 oz) can or bottle beer (not too dark or bitter)
- 2 tbsp. honey or agave, warmed
- 6 tbsp. butter, melted

Directions:

1. Supply your smoker with wood pellets and follow the start-up procedure. Preheat the grill, with the lid closed, to 350° F.

2. Lightly grease a 9 ×5 inch loaf pan.

3. In a large mixing bowl, put in the flour, sugar, baking powder, and salt. Whisk to combine and aerate, using a wire whisk. Add the beer and honey and stir with a wooden spoon until the batter is properly mixed (Do not over-mix).

4. Pour half of the melted butter into the prepared loaf pan and pour in the batter. Pour the remaining butter over the top of the loaf.

5. Place the loaf pan on the grill grate and bake for 50 to 60 minutes or until the bread is golden brown.

6. Allow the loaf to cool slightly in the pan before removing it from the pan. Leftovers make great toast.

Green Bean Casserole Circa 1955

Servings: 6

Cooking Time: 30 Minutes

Ingredients:

- ➢ 1 1/2 Pound Green Beans, fresh
- ➢ 1 Can cream of mushroom soup
- ➢ 1/2 Cup milk
- ➢ 2 Teaspoon soy sauce
- ➢ 1/2 Teaspoon Worcestershire sauce
- ➢ 1/2 Teaspoon black pepper
- ➢ 1.334 Cup French's Original Crispy Fried Onions
- ➢ 1/4 Cup red bell pepper, diced

Directions:

1. In a mixing bowl, combine the beans (trimmed and cooked until tender, or may use 2 16 oz. cans), soup, milk, soy sauce, Worcestershire sauce, black pepper, 2/3 cup of the onion rings, and red pepper, if using. Transfer to a 1-1/2 quart casserole dish.

2. Supply your smoker with wood pellets and follow the start-up procedure. Preheat the grill, with the lid closed, to 375° F.

3. Cook the casserole until the filling is hot and bubbling, 25 to 30 minutes. Top with the remaining onions and cook for 5 to 10 minutes more, or until the onions are crisp and beginning to brown. Grill: 375 °F

Skillet Buttermilk Cornbread

Servings: 6

Cooking Time: 25 Minutes

Ingredients:

- 1 Cup Cornmeal
- 1 Cup all-purpose flour
- 1/3 Cup granulated sugar
- 1 Teaspoon salt
- 1 Teaspoon baking powder
- 1 1/2 Cup buttermilk
- 2 Whole eggs
- 8 Tablespoon butter, melted

Directions:

1. Grease a cast iron skillet or 9-inch square baking pan with bacon fat. Put a 10-inch well-seasoned cast iron skillet on the grill grate. If using a regular baking pan, do not preheat.

2. Supply your smoker with wood pellets and follow the start-up procedure. Preheat the grill, with the lid closed, to 400° F.

3. In a large mixing bowl, combine the cornmeal, flour, sugar, salt, and baking powder and whisk to mix thoroughly. Make a well in the center of the dry ingredients.

4. In a separate mixing bowl, whisk together the buttermilk and eggs until well-combined. Add the melted butter. Pour into the dry ingredients and mix until the batter is fairly smooth. Do not overmix.

5. Carefully pour the batter into the preheated skillet. Bake for 20 to 25 minutes, or until the top is firm and a tester inserted in the center of the cornbread comes out clean. Be careful when removing the skillet from the grill as it will be very hot. Let the cornbread cool slightly on a trivet or cooling rack before slicing into wedges or squares.

SEAFOOD RECIPES

Sweet Smoked Salmon Jerky

Servings: 6

Cooking Time: 300 Minutes

Ingredients:

- 2 Quart water
- 3/4 Cup kosher salt
- 1 Cup Morton Tender Quick Home Meat Cure, optional
- 4 Cup dark brown sugar
- 2 Cup maple syrup, divided
- 1 (2-3 lb) wild caught salmon fillet, skinned and pin bones removed

Directions:

1. In a large nonreactive bowl, combine 2 quarts water, salt, curing salt (if using), brown sugar and 1 cup of the maple syrup. Stir with a long-handled spoon to dissolve the salts and sugar.

2. With a sharp, serrated knife, slice the salmon into 1/2 inch thick slices with the short side parallel to you on the cutting board. In other words, make your cuts from the head end to the tail end. (This is considerably easier if the fish is frozen.) Cut each strip crosswise into 4 or 5 inch lengths.

3. Immerse the strips in the brine, weighing down with a plate or a bag of ice. Cover with plastic wrap and refrigerate for 12 hours.

4. Supply your smoker with wood pellets and follow the start-up procedure. Preheat the grill, with the lid closed, to 180° F.

5. Drain the salmon strips and discard the brine. Arrange the salmon strips in a single layer directly on the grill grate. Smoke for several hours (5 to 6), or until the jerky is dry but not rock-hard. You want it to yield when you bite into it. Halfway through the smoking time, mix the remaining cup of maple syrup with 1/4 cup of warm water and brush the salmon strips on all sides with the mixture. Grill: 180 °F

6. Transfer to a resealable bag while the jerky is still warm. Let the jerky rest for an hour at room temperature. Squeeze any air from the bag, and refrigerate the jerky. Enjoy!

Grilled Lemon Salmon

Servings: 4

Cooking Time: 60 Minutes

Ingredients:

➢ Dill, Fresh

➢ 1 Lemon, Sliced

➢ 1 1/2 - 2 Lbs Salmon, Fresh

Directions:

1. Supply your smoker with wood pellets and follow the start-up procedure. Preheat the grill, with the lid closed, to 225° F.

2. Place the salmon on a cedar plank. Lay the lemon slices along the top of the salmon. Smoke in your Grill for about 60 minutes.

3. Top with fresh dill and serve.

Grilled Lemon Shrimp Scampi

Servings: 4

Cooking Time: 6 Minutes

Ingredients:

- ➢ 1 ½ pounds medium shrimp, peeled and deveined
- ➢ ¼ cup olive oil
- ➢ ¼ cup lemon juice
- ➢ 3 tablespoons chopped fresh parsley
- ➢ 1 tablespoon minced garlic
- ➢ ground black pepper to taste
- ➢ ¼ teaspoon crushed red pepper flakes to taste

Directions:

1. In a large, non-reactive bowl, stir together the olive oil, lemon juice, parsley, garlic, and black pepper. Season with crushed red pepper, if desired. Add shrimp, and toss to coat. Marinate in the refrigerator for 30 minutes.

2. Supply your smoker with wood pellets and follow the start-up procedure. Preheat the grill, with the lid closed, to high heat.

3. Thread shrimp onto skewers, piercing once near the tail and once near the head. Discard any remaining marinade.

4. Lightly oil grill grate. Place the shrimp skewers on the grill grates.

5. Grill for 2 to 3 minutes per side, or until opaque.

Simple Glazed Salmon Fillets

Servings: 2

Cooking Time: 25 Minutes

Ingredients:

- 4 (6-8 oz) center-cut salmon fillets, skin on
- Fin & Feather Rub
- 1/2 Cup mayonnaise
- 2 Tablespoon Dijon mustard
- 1 Tablespoon fresh lemon juice
- 1 Tablespoon fresh chopped tarragon or dill
- lemon wedges

Directions:

1. Season the fillets with the Traeger Fin & Feather Rub.

2. Make the Glaze: Combine the mayonnaise and mustard in a small bowl. Stir in the lemon juice and dill or tarragon.

3. Spread the flesh-side of the fillets with the glaze.

4. Supply your smoker with wood pellets and follow the start-up procedure. Preheat the grill, with the lid closed, to 350° F.

5. Arrange the salmon fillets on the grill grate, skin-side down. Grill for 25 to 30 minutes, or until the salmon is opaque and flakes easily with a fork. Grill: 350 °F

6. Transfer to a platter or plates, garnish with sliced lemons and chopped dill and serve immediately. Enjoy!

Grilled Albacore Tuna With Potato-tomato Casserole

Servings: 8

Cooking Time: 20 Minutes

Ingredients:

- 6 Tuna Steaks, 6oz
- 1 Whole lemon zest
- 1 chile de árbol, thinly sliced
- 1 Tablespoon thyme
- 1 Tablespoon fresh parsley

Directions:

1. To make the fish: Season the fish with the lemon zest, chile, thyme, and parsley. Cover and refrigerate at least 4 hours.

2. Remove fish from the refrigerator 30 minutes before cooking to come to room temperature.

3. Season the fish with salt and pepper on both sides. Grill 2-3 minutes per side (next to the cast iron with the casserole) rotating it once or twice. The tuna should be well seared but still rare.

Lemon Herb Grilled Salmon

Servings: 4

Cooking Time: 25 Minutes

Ingredients:

- 1 1/2 pounds salmon with skin
- 1/2 tablespoon lemon zest
- 1 tablespoon lemon juice
- 1 tablespoon unsalted butter
- 1/2 teaspoon sea salt
- 1/2 teaspoon ground black pepper
- 2 teaspoons freshly chopped dill
- 1 teaspoon freshly chopped parsley
- lemon slices for the garnish

Directions:

1. Supply your smoker with wood pellets and follow the start-up procedure. Preheat the grill, with the lid closed, to 325° F.

2. In a small bowl, combine the lemon zest, lemon juice, softened unsalted butter, dill, parsley, sea salt, and ground black pepper.

3. Generously slather the top of the salmon fillet with the mixture and top with a slice of lemon. You may allow marinating for about 10 minutes or so to absorb the mixture.

4. Place the salmon fillets on the hot grill grate, skin-side facing down.

5. Cook the salmon for 20 to 25 minutes, until it reaches an internal temperature of 145 °F and flakes easily, or until the salmon is cooked to your preferred taste.

6. Serve with lemon slices. Enjoy!

Moules Marinières With Garlic Butter Sauce

Servings: 4

Cooking Time: 12 Minutes

Ingredients:

- 3lb (1.4kg) fresh mussels, scrubbed under cold running water and debearded
- lemon wedges
- crusty bread (optional)
- for the sauce
- 6 tbsp unsalted butter
- 3 garlic cloves, peeled and minced
- 1 cup dry white wine or hard cider
- 1 tbsp freshly squeezed lemon juice
- 2 tsp hot sauce, plus more
- coarse salt
- freshly ground black pepper
- 2 tbsp chopped fresh curly parsley or tarragon

Directions:

1. Supply your smoker with wood pellets and follow the start-up procedure. Preheat the grill, with the lid closed, to 450° F.

2. In a small saucepan on the stovetop over medium-low heat, make the sauce by melting the butter. Add the garlic and sauté for 1 to 2 minutes. Add the wine, lemon juice, and hot sauce. Season with salt and pepper to taste. Simmer for 5 minutes. Remove the saucepan from the heat and stir in the parsley. Keep warm.

3. Discard any mussels that are cracked or don't snap shut when tapped. Place the mussels in a large aluminum foil roasting pan and cover tightly with heavy-duty aluminum foil.

4. Place the pan on the grate and steam the mussels until the shells open, about 10 to 12 minutes. Remove the pan from the grill and use long-handled tongs to remove the foil from the pan. (Be careful of escaping steam.) Use the tongs to discard any mussels that don't open.

5. Pour the reserved garlic butter sauce over the mussels. Serve from the pan or transfer the mussels to a shallow serving bowl. Serve immediately with lemon wedges, additional hot sauce, and crusty bread (if using) to sop up the juices.

Smoked Honey Salmon

Servings: 2

Cooking Time: 25 Minutes

Ingredients:

- 1 lb. salmon fillets
- 1/2 tsp. pepper
- 1/4 tsp. salt
- 2 tbsp. sriracha
- 2 tsp. honey
- 2 tsp. chili sauce
- 1 tsp. lime juice
- 1/2 tsp. fish sauce

Directions:

1. Supply your smoker with wood pellets and follow the start-up procedure. Preheat the grill, with the lid closed, to 350° F.
2. Sprinkle the salmon with salt and pepper.
3. In a bowl, whisk together the sriracha, honey, chili sauce, lime juice, and fish sauce.
4. Once the grill is hot, place the salmon on the grill and leave for 15 minutes.
5. After 15 minutes, brush the salmon with the sriracha chili sauce and keep cooking for 5-10minutes. The salmon should be firm to the touch and crispy on the edges.
6. Serve hot!

Smoked Sugar Halibut

Servings: 8

Cooking Time: 120 Minutes

Ingredients:

- ➢ 1/4 cup granulated sugar
- ➢ 1/4 cup brown sugar
- ➢ 1/2 cup kosher salt
- ➢ 1 tsp ground coriander
- ➢ 2 lbs fresh halibut

Directions:

1. In a small bowl, mix the sugars, salt,and coriander together. Season the halibut on all sides.

2. Wrap the halibut in plastic wrap, place on a rimmed sheet pan,and brine in the fridge for 3 hours.

3. Remove the plastic wrap and rinse the fish. Pat it dry. Set it on a drying rack over a sheet pan for 1-2 hours in the fridge.

4. Supply your smoker with wood pellets and follow the start-up procedure. Preheat the grill, with the lid closed, to 200° F. Smoke the fish for 2 hours or until its internal temperature reaches 140 °F.

5. Serve your preferred sauce with the fish.

Traeger Smoked Salmon

Servings: 6

Cooking Time: 240 Minutes

Ingredients:

- 1 (2-1/2 to 3 lb) salmon fillet
- 1/2 Cup kosher salt
- 1 Cup brown sugar, firmly packed
- 1 Tablespoon ground black pepper

Directions:

1. Remove all pin bones from salmon.

2. In a small bowl, combine salt, sugar and black pepper. Lay a large piece of plastic wrap on a flat surface that is at least 6 inches longer than the fillet. Spread 1/2 of the mixture on top of the plastic and lay the fillet skin side down on top of the cure. Top with the other 1/2 of the cure spreading it evenly over the top of the fillet. Fold up the edges of the plastic and wrap tightly.

3. Place the wrapped salmon fillet in the bottom of a flat, rectangle baking dish or hotel pan. Place another identical pan on top of the fillet. Place a couple of cans or something heavy inside the top pan to weigh it down making sure the weight is distributed evenly.

4. Transfer the weighted salmon to the refrigerator and cure for 4 to 6 hours.

5. Remove the salmon from the plastic wrap and rinse the cure thoroughly (not rinsing thoroughly will result in a salty finished product). Place skin side down on a wire rack atop a sheet tray and pat dry. Place the sheet tray in the refrigerator and allow the salmon to dry overnight. This allows a tacky film called a pellicle to form on the surface of the salmon. The pellicle helps smoke adhere to the fish.

6. Supply your smoker with wood pellets and follow the start-up procedure. Preheat the grill, with the lid closed, to 180° F.

7. Place the salmon skin side down directly on the grill grate and smoke for 3 to 4 hours or until the internal temperature of the fish registers 140°F. Enjoy warm or chilled. Grill: 180 °F Probe: 140 °F

Cajun-blackened Shrimp

Servings: 4

Cooking Time: 20 Minutes

Ingredients:

- ➤ 1 pound peeled and deveined shrimp, with tails on
- ➤ 1 batch Cajun Rub
- ➤ 8 tablespoons (1 stick) butter
- ➤ ¼ cup Worcestershire sauce

Directions:

1. Supply your smoker with wood pellets and follow the start-up procedure. Preheat the grill, with the lid closed, to 450°F and place a cast-iron skillet on the grill grate. Wait about 10 minutes after your grill has reached temperature, allowing the skillet to get hot.

2. Meanwhile, season the shrimp all over with the rub.

3. When the skillet is hot, place the butter in it to melt. Once the butter melts, stir in the Worcestershire sauce.

4. Add the shrimp and gently stir to coat. Smoke-braise the shrimp for about 10 minutes per side, until opaque and cooked through. Remove the shrimp from the grill and serve immediately.

Spicy Crab Poppers

Servings: 8

Cooking Time: 30 Minutes

Ingredients:

- 18 Whole jalapeño
- 8 Ounce cream cheese, softened
- 1 Cup Canned Corn, drained
- 1/2 Cup Crab meat, lump
- 1 1/4 Teaspoon Old Bay Seasoning
- 2 Scallions, minced

Directions:

1. Cut each jalapeño in half lengthwise through the stem and remove the ribs and seeds.

2. Filling: In a mixing bowl, combine the cream cheese, corn, crab meat, scallions, and Old Bay Seasoning and stir until blended. Stir in the scallions. Spoon the filling into the jalapeño halves, mounding it slightly.

3. Arrange the poppers on a baking sheet covered with foil or parchment paper.

4. Supply your smoker with wood pellets and follow the start-up procedure. Preheat the grill, with the lid closed, to 350° F.

5. Roast the jalapeños for 25 to 30 minutes, or until the peppers have softened and the filling is hot and bubbling.

6. Let cool slightly before serving. Enjoy!

Lemon Shrimp Scampi

Servings: 3

Cooking Time: 10 Minutes

Ingredients:

- 2 Tsp Blackened Sriracha Rub Seasoning
- 1/2 Cup Butter, Cubed, Divided
- 1/2 Tsp Chili Pepper Flakes
- 3 Garlic Cloves, Minced
- To Taste, Lemon Wedges, For Serving
- 1 Lemon, Juice & Zest
- Linguine, Cooked
- 3 Tbsp Parsley, Chopped
- 1 1/2 Lbs Shrimp, Peeled & Deveined
- Toasted Baguette, For Serving

Directions:

1. Supply your smoker with wood pellets and follow the start-up procedure. Preheat the grill, with the lid closed, to medium-high heat. If using a gas or charcoal grill, set it up for medium-high heat.

2. Add half of the butter to the griddle, then sauté the garlic, Blackened Sriracha, and chili flakes for 1 minute, until fragrant.

3. Add the shrimp, turning occasionally for 2 minutes, until opaque.

4. Add the remaining butter, parsley, lemon zest and juice. Toss the shrimp to coat in lemon butter, then remove from the griddle, and transfer to a serving bowl.

5. Serve immediately, with fresh lemon wedges, and toasted baguette. Serve over linguine, spaghetti or zucchini noodles, if desired.

VEGETABLES RECIPES

Roasted Tomatoes

Servings: 2

Cooking Time: 180 Minutes

Ingredients:

- 3 Large ripe tomatoes
- 1/2 Tablespoon kosher salt
- 1 Teaspoon coarse ground black pepper
- 1/4 Teaspoon sugar
- 1/4 Teaspoon thyme or basil
- olive oil

Directions:

1. Line a rimmed baking sheet with parchment paper.

2. Supply your smoker with wood pellets and follow the start-up procedure. Preheat the grill, with the lid closed, to 225° F.

3. Remove the stem end from each tomato and cut the tomatoes into 1/2 inch thick slices.

4. Combine the salt, pepper, sugar and thyme or basil in a small bowl and mix.

5. Pour olive oil into the well of a dinner plate.

6. Dip one side of each tomato slice in the olive oil and arrange on the baking sheet. Dust the tomato slices with the seasoning mixture.

7. Arrange the pan directly on the grill grate and roast the tomatoes until the juices stop running and the edges have contracted, about 3 hours. Remove from grill and enjoy!

Butternut Squash

Servings: 4

Cooking Time: 45 Minutes

Ingredients:

- ➢ 1 Whole butternut squash
- ➢ Veggie Rub
- ➢ Blackened Saskatchewan Rub
- ➢ olive oil

Directions:

1. Cut squash in half and lightly coat with mixture of olive oil, Traeger Veggie Shake, and Traeger Blackened Saskatchewan.

2. Wrap in foil with 1/2 cup (120mL) of water.

3. Supply your smoker with wood pellets and follow the start-up procedure. Preheat the grill, with the lid closed, to 450° F.

4. Place squash on grill for 45 minutes. Remove from grill and unwrap. Enjoy!

Baked Sweet And Savory Yams By Bennie Kendrick

Servings: 6

Cooking Time: 60 Minutes

Ingredients:

- 3 Medium Yams
- 3 Tablespoon extra-virgin olive oil
- honey
- Goat Cheese
- 1/2 Cup brown sugar
- 1/2 Cup Pecans, pieces

Directions:

1. Supply your smoker with wood pellets and follow the start-up procedure. Preheat the grill, with the lid closed, to 350° F.

2. While Traeger comes to temperature, wash yams and poke a few holes all over. Wrap yams in foil.

3. Bake for 45-60 minutes or until knife tender. You don't want to overcook and get the yams too soft because you want to be able to cut each yam into rounds.

4. Once yams have cooled to the touch, cut each into 1/4" rounds. Lightly coat each round with oil olive and place on sheet tray.

5. Sprinkle each top with brown sugar. Using a teaspoon, place desired amount of goat cheese on each round. Next top with chopped pecans. Finally, drizzle Bee Local honey over each round.

6. Based on how sweet you like your yams, you can add more brown sugar and honey.

7. After complete, place your sheet tray back in the grill and cook, lid closed, for another 20 minutes. Enjoy!

Christmas Brussel Sprouts

Servings: 6

Cooking Time: 50 Minutes

Ingredients:

- 1/2 Pound thick-cut bacon
- 1 Medium onion, diced
- 2 Pound fresh Brussels sprouts
- 2 Tablespoon olive oil
- salt and pepper

Directions:

1. Supply your smoker with wood pellets and follow the start-up procedure. Preheat the grill, with the lid closed, to 350° F.

2. Place bacon directly on grill grate and cook for 15-20 minutes, or until lightly browned. Remove from grill and set aside on paper towel lined plate.

3. Slice onion in half and then slice into 1/4 inch moons and add to large mixing bowl. Slice brussels sprouts in half lengthwise and add to bowl.

4. Cut reserved bacon into 1/2 inch pieces and add to bowl. Drizzle with olive oil and sprinkle with salt and pepper. Toss to coat and pour into baking pan.

5. Turn the temperature on grill to 375 and place baking pan on grill. Roast for 30 minutes mixing halfway through cooking. Grill: 375 °F

Roasted Jalapeño Poppers

Servings: 2

Cooking Time: 30 Minutes

Ingredients:

- 8 Slices Bacon, Center Cut
- 2 Cup cream cheese
- 2 Ounce Cheese, sharp cheddar
- 1/2 Cup green onions, minced
- 2 Teaspoon fresh squeezed lime juice
- 4 Tablespoon Seeded Tomato, Chopped
- 4 Tablespoon cilantro, chopped
- 1/2 Teaspoon kosher salt
- 2 Small garlic clove, minced
- 12 Whole Jalapeños

Directions:

1. Supply your smoker with wood pellets and follow the start-up procedure. Preheat the grill, with the lid closed, to 350° F.

2. Place 2 bacon slices directly on the grill grate and cook 10-15 minutes until cooked through and crispy flipping halfway through. Remove from grill, but leave the grill on. When cool enough to handle, coarsely chop the bacon and reserve. Grill: 350 ˚F

3. In the bowl of a stand mixer, combine cream cheese, cheddar cheese, green onions, chopped bacon, lime juice, tomatoes, cilantro, salt and garlic. Mix on medium speed with a paddle until combined. Transfer mixture to a piping bag.

4. Cut the tops off the jalapeños and remove the seeds and ribs with a small paring knife.

5. Pipe the filling into each pepper so that the filling comes up a 1/4" over the top of the pepper. Place the tops back on each pepper.

6. With a rolling pin, flatten out the remaining six slices of bacon until they are 1/8" thick. Cut each slice in half. Wrap 1/2 a bacon slice around each pepper and secure with a toothpick.

7. Place the peppers in the Traeger Jalapeno Popper Tray. Place the tray directly on the grill grate and cook for 30-40 minutes until the peppers are tender, bacon is crispy, and cheese is melted. Enjoy! Grill: 350 ˚F

Salt Crusted Baked Potatoes

Servings: 4

Cooking Time: 60 Minutes

Ingredients:

- 6 russet potatoes, scrubbed and dried
- 3 Tablespoon canola oil
- 1 Tablespoon kosher salt
- butter
- sour cream
- Chives, fresh
- Bacon Bits
- cheddar cheese

Directions:

1. In a large bowl, coat the potatoes in canola oil and sprinkle heavily with salt.

2. Supply your smoker with wood pellets and follow the start-up procedure. Preheat the grill, with the lid closed, to 450° F.

3. Place the potatoes directly on the grill grate and bake for 30-40 minutes, or until soft in the middle when pricked with a fork. Serve loaded with your favorite toppings. Enjoy! Grill: 450 °F

Spicy Asian Brussels Sprouts

Servings: 4

Cooking Time: 10 Minutes

Ingredients:

- ➢ 2 Cup fresh Brussels sprouts
- ➢ 2 Tablespoon vegetable oil
- ➢ 1 Tablespoon Asian BBQ Rub
- ➢ 1/4 Cup Thai sweet chile sauce

Directions:

1. Supply your smoker with wood pellets and follow the start-up procedure. Preheat the grill, with the lid closed, to 350° F.

2. Spread the halved brussel sprouts in a single layer on a lined cookie sheet. Drizzle with the oil and toss to coat.

3. Sprinkle the brussel sprouts evenly with an Asian BBQ rub and put the cookie sheet on the grill. Close the lid and cook for 7-8 minutes. Grill: 350 ˚F

4. Toss the brussels sprouts in the Thai Chili Sauce and return to the grill for an additional 3-4 minutes, or until the sprouts are crisp-tender. Grill: 350 ˚F

5. Serve immediately. Enjoy!

Grilled Fingerling Potato Salad

Servings: 6

Cooking Time: 15 Minutes

Ingredients:

- ➢ 10 Whole scallions
- ➢ 2/3 Cup extra-virgin olive oil, divided
- ➢ 1 1/2 Pound fingerling potatoes, cut in half lengthwise
- ➢ pepper
- ➢ 2 Teaspoon kosher salt, divided, plus more as needed
- ➢ 2 Tablespoon rice vinegar
- ➢ 2 Teaspoon lemon juice
- ➢ 1 Small jalapeño, sliced

Directions:

1. Supply your smoker with wood pellets and follow the start-up procedure. Preheat the grill, with the lid closed, to 450° F.

2. Brush the scallions with oil and place on the grill.

3. Cook until lightly charred, about 2 to 3 minutes. Remove and let cool. Grill: 450 ˚F

4. Once the scallions have cooled, slice and set aside.

5. Brush the fingerling potatoes with oil (reserving 1/3 cup for later use), then salt and pepper. Place cut-side down on the grill until cooked through, about 4 to 5 minutes. Grill: 450 ˚F

6. In a bowl, whisk the remaining 1/3 cup olive oil, 1 teaspoon salt, rice vinegar and lemon juice. Next mix in the scallions, potatoes and sliced jalapeño.

7. Season with salt and pepper, and serve. Enjoy!

Roasted Hasselback Potatoes By Doug Scheiding

Servings: 6

Cooking Time: 120 Minutes

Ingredients:

- 6 Large russet potatoes
- 1 Pound bacon
- 1/2 Cup butter
- salt
- black pepper
- 1 Cup cheddar cheese
- 3 Whole scallions

Directions:

1. To cut potatoes, place two wooden spoons on either side of the potato (this prevents your knife from going all the way through). Slice potato into thin chips leaving about 1/4" attached on the bottom.

2. Freeze bacon slices for about 30 minutes then cut into small pieces about the size of a stamp. Place these in the cracks between every other slice.

3. Place the potato in a large cast iron skillet. Top the potato with slices of hard butter (you can also place thin slivers of cold butter between the potato slices with the bacon if desired). Season with salt and pepper.

4. Supply your smoker with wood pellets and follow the start-up procedure. Preheat the grill, with the lid closed, to 350° F.

5. Place the cast iron directly on the grill grate and cook for two hours. Top potatoes with more butter and baste with melted butter every 30 minutes.

6. In the last 10 minutes of cooking, sprinkle with cheddar and return to grill to melt.

7. To finish, top with chives or scallions. Enjoy!

Grilled Corn On The Cob With Parmesan And Garlic

Servings: 6

Cooking Time: 30 Minutes

Ingredients:

- 4 Tablespoon butter, melted
- 2 Clove garlic, minced
- salt and pepper
- 8 ears fresh corn
- 1/2 Cup shaved Parmesan
- 1 Tablespoon chopped parsley

Directions:

1. Supply your smoker with wood pellets and follow the start-up procedure. Preheat the grill, with the lid closed, to 450° F.

2. Place butter, garlic, salt and pepper in a medium bowl and mix well.

3. Peel back corn husks and remove the silk. Rub corn with half of the garlic butter mixture.

4. Close husks and place directly on the grill grate. Cook for 25 to 30 minutes, turning occasionally until corn is tender. Grill: 450 ˚F

5. Remove from grill, peel and discard husks. Place corn on serving tray, drizzle with remaining butter and top with Parmesan and parsley.

Steak Fries With Horseradish Creme

Servings: 6

Cooking Time: 25 Minutes

Ingredients:

➢ 5 Potatoes, Baking

➢ 2 Tablespoon extra-virgin olive oil

➢ 1 Teaspoon butter

➢ 3 Clove garlic, crushed

➢ 1 Teaspoon onion powder

➢ 2 Teaspoon Jacobsen Salt Co. Pure Kosher Sea Salt

➢ 1 Teaspoon black pepper

Directions:

1. Wash the potatoes thoroughly, and cut them in eighths, then toss them in the olive oil, butter, crushed garlic, onion powder, salt, and pepper.

2. Supply your smoker with wood pellets and follow the start-up procedure. Preheat the grill, with the lid closed, to 450° F.

3. In order to get great grill marks, line up the wedges on the front of the grill and the back of the grill, turning to get grill marks on all sides.

4. Once they have been seared, move them to the center of the grill and finish cooking about ten more minutes, serve hot with the horseradish mayo. Enjoy!

Baked Artichoke Parmesan Mushrooms

Servings: 8

Cooking Time: 30 Minutes

Ingredients:

- 8 Cremini Mushroom Caps
- 6 1/2 Ounce artichoke hearts
- 1/3 Cup Parmesan cheese, grated
- 1/4 Cup mayonnaise
- 1/2 Teaspoon garlic salt
- your favorite hot sauce
- paprika

Directions:

1. Clean the mushrooms with a damp paper towel. Remove the stems and discard or save for another use.

2. Using a small spoon, scoop out the inside (gills, etc.). Combine the artichoke hearts, parmesan, mayonnaise, garlic salt, and hot sauce and mix well.

3. Mound the filling in the mushroom caps. Dust the tops with paprika.

4. Arrange the mushrooms in an oven-safe baking dish.

5. Supply your smoker with wood pellets and follow the start-up procedure. Preheat the grill, with the lid closed, to 350° F.

6. Bake the mushrooms (uncovered) until the filling is bubbling and just beginning to brown, about 25 to 30 minutes. Serve immediately. Grill: 350 °F

7. For a simple variation, stuff the mushrooms with your favorite bulk sausage and bake on your Traeger as directed above. Enjoy!

Skillet Potato Cake

Servings: 4

Cooking Time: 40 Minutes

Ingredients:

- ➢ 8 Tablespoon butter, melted
- ➢ 2 Pound russet potatoes, peeled and thinly sliced
- ➢ 3 Tablespoon kosher salt
- ➢ 2 Tablespoon freshly ground black pepper
- ➢ thyme

Directions:

1. Supply your smoker with wood pellets and follow the start-up procedure. Preheat the grill, with the lid closed, to 375° F.

2. Brush the bottom of a cast iron skillet with part of the melted butter. Place potato slices vertically around the outer edges then fill in the middle in the same fashion.

3. Pour additional melted butter over the top of the layers and sprinkle with salt and pepper.

4. Place skillet in grill and cook for 35 to 40 minutes or until potatoes are fork tender and golden brown.

5. Garnish with a sprinkle of fresh thyme over the top of the potatoes. Enjoy!

POULTRY RECIPES

Roasted Christmas Goose

Servings: 8

Cooking Time: 120 Minutes

Ingredients:

- ➢ 5 1/2 Pound Goose
- ➢ 2 lemons
- ➢ 2 limes
- ➢ 2 Teaspoon salt
- ➢ 2 thyme sprigs
- ➢ 2 sage sprigs
- ➢ 1 Medium Apple, green
- ➢ 3 Tablespoon honey

Directions:

1. Supply your smoker with wood pellets and follow the start-up procedure. Preheat the grill, with the lid closed, to High heat.

2. Lightly score the breast and leg skin in a criss-cross pattern. This will help the fat to render down more quickly during cooking.

3. Grate the lemon and limes. Mix citrus zest with 2 teaspoons fine sea salt. Cut the lemons and lime into wedges.

4. Season cavity of the goose generously with salt, then rub the citrus mix well into the skin and sprinkle some inside the cavity.

5. Stuff goose with sage, thyme, lemons, limes and apples wedges. Place goose directly on the grill grate and cook for 40 minutes. Brush goose with honey and reduce temperature to 325°F.

6. Cook for 1-1/2 to 2 hours or until an instant read thermometer inserted in the thickest part of the breast reads 160°F. Grill: 325 °F Probe: 160 °F

7. Remove from grill, tent with foil and allow to rest for 30 minutes. Final internal temperature should be 165°F in the thickest part of the breast. Enjoy!

Smoked Turkey Wings

Servings: 2

Cooking Time: 60 Minutes

Ingredients:

➢   4 turkey wings

➢   1 batch Sweet and Spicy Cinnamon Rub

Directions:

1.   Supply your smoker with wood pellets and follow the start-up procedure. Preheat the grill, with the lid closed, to 180°F.

2.   Using your hands, work the rub into the turkey wings, coating them completely.

3.   Place the wings directly on the grill grate and cook for 30 minutes.

4.   Increase the grill's temperature to 325°F and continue to cook until the turkey's internal temperature reaches 170°F. Remove the wings from the grill and serve immediately.

Spiced Smoked Chicken Quarters

Servings: 4

Cooking Time: 120 Minutes

Ingredients:

- ➢ 4 chicken leg quarters
- ➢ For the rub:
- ➢ 2 tbsp paprika
- ➢ 1 tbsp thyme
- ➢ 2 tbsp chili powder
- ➢ 2 tbsp cayenne pepper
- ➢ 1 tbsp garlic powder
- ➢ 1 tbsp onion powder
- ➢ 1 tbsp kosher/table salt
- ➢ 2 tbsp black pepper
- ➢ 1 tbsp olive oil

Directions:

1. Supply your smoker with wood pellets and follow the start-up procedure. Preheat the grill, with the lid closed, to 220° F.

2. Pat down chicken pieces with a paper towel to make them dry. Cut off any excess fat that's visible on the outside of the meat.

3. Apply a thin layer of oil to the chicken skin. In a small bowl, combine all the BBQ rub ingredients thoroughly. Apply BBQ rub generously to your chicken thighs, rubbing in firmly and thoroughly.

4. Transfer chicken quarters to your smoker rack.Close the lid.

5. Cook until the quarters reach an internal temperature of 165°F, about 2 hours.

6. Once cooked, increase the grill temperature to medium heat. Cook for just a few minutes, turning regularly, for a crispy skin.

Roasted Whole Chicken

Servings: 6-8

Cooking Time: 120 Minutes

Ingredients:

- 1 whole chicken
- 2 tablespoons olive oil
- 1 batch Chicken Rub

Directions:

1. Supply your smoker with wood pellets and follow the start-up procedure. Preheat the grill, with the lid closed, to 375°F.

2. Coat the chicken all over with olive oil and season it with the rub. Using your hands, work the rub into the meat.

3. Place the chicken directly on the grill grate and smoke until its internal temperature reaches 170°F.

4. Remove the chicken from the grill and let it rest for 10 minutes, before carving and serving.

Savory Cajun Bbq Chicken

Servings: 4

Cooking Time: 25 Minutes

Ingredients:

- ½ Cup Barbecue Sauce
- ¼ Cup Beer, Any Brand
- 1 Tablespoon Butter
- 1 Pound Boneless, Skinless Chicken Breasts
- 2 Cloves Garlic Clove, Minced
- ¼ Teaspoon Ground Thyme
- 1 Teaspoon Hot Sauce
- Juice Of 1 Lime
- 1 Tablespoon Olive Oil
- ½ Teaspoon Oregano
- 2 Tablespoons Sweet Heat Rub
- 1 Tablespoon Worcestershire Sauce

Directions:

1. In a small mixing bowl, mix together the Sweet Heat Rub, oregano, and ground thyme.

2. Rub the chicken breasts all over with olive oil, making sure to completely coat the meat. Generously season the chicken breasts on all sides with the Sweet Heat mixture.

3. Supply your smoker with wood pellets and follow the start-up procedure. Preheat the grill, with the lid closed, to 350° F. If you're using a gas or charcoal grill, set it up for medium heat. Insert a temperature probe into the thickest part of one of the chicken breasts and place the meat on the grill. Grill the meat on one side for 10-12 minutes, then flip and grill for another 5-7 minutes, or until the chicken breasts are golden brown and juicy and reaches an internal temperature of 165°F.

4. Remove the chicken from the grill and allow to rest for 10 minutes.

5. While the chicken rests, make the sauce. Combine the butter, barbecue sauce, beer, Worcestershire sauce, lime juice, and minced garlic in a heat proof saucepan and place on the grill. Bring the sauce to a boil. Once it boils, remove it from the heat, whisk it and serve with the chicken.

Turkey & Bacon Kebabs With Ranch-style Dressing

Servings: 8　　　　　　　　　　　　　Cooking Time: 25 Minutes

Ingredients:

- 1½lb (680g) skinless turkey tenders or boneless, skinless turkey breasts, cut into 1-inch (2.5cm) chunks
- 8 strips of thick-cut bacon
- 12 fresh bay leaves (optional)
- for the dressing
- 1 cup reduced-fat mayo
- 1 cup light sour cream
- ½ cup buttermilk or whole milk, plus more
- 2 tbsp minced fresh parsley
- 2 tbsp minced fresh chives
- 1 tbsp minced fresh dill
- 2 tsp freshly squeezed lemon juice
- 1 tsp Worcestershire sauce
- 1 tsp garlic salt
- 1 tsp onion powder
- ½ tsp coarse salt, plus more
- ½ tsp freshly ground black pepper, plus more

Directions:

1. In a large bowl, make the dressing by whisking together the mayo, sour cream, and buttermilk until smooth. Whisk in the remaining ingredients. Pour half the mixture into a small bowl. Cover and refrigerate.

2. Add the turkey to the mixture remaining in the bowl and toss to coat thoroughly. If the dressing seems too thick (dip-like), add more buttermilk 1 tablespoon at a time. Cover and refrigerate for 2 to 4 hours.

3. Supply your smoker with wood pellets and follow the start-up procedure. Preheat the grill, with the lid closed, to 375° F.

4. Place the bacon on the grate and cook until some of the fat has rendered and the bacon begins to brown, about 15 minutes. Remove the bacon from the grill to cool. Cut the bacon into 1-inch (2.5cm) squares. Set aside.

5. Drain the tenders and discard any excess dressing. Alternate threading the turkey, bacon pieces, and 3 bay leaves on a bamboo skewer. Repeat the threading with 3 more skewers.

6. Place the kebabs on the grate and grill until the turkey is cooked through, about 4 to 5 minutes per side, turning as needed.

7. Transfer the skewers to a platter. Serve with the reserved dressing.

Wild West Wings

Servings: 4

Cooking Time: 60 Minutes

Ingredients:

➢ 2 pounds chicken wings

➢ 2 tablespoons extra-virgin olive oil

➢ 2 packages ranch dressing mix (such as Hidden Valley brand)

➢ ¼ cup prepared ranch dressing (optional)

Directions:

1. Supply your smoker with wood pellets and follow the start-up procedure. Preheat, with the lid closed, to 350°F.

2. Place the chicken wings in a large bowl and toss with the olive oil and ranch dressing mix.

3. Arrange the wings directly on the grill, or line the grill with aluminum foil for easy cleanup, close the lid, and smoke for 25 minutes.

4. Flip and smoke for 20 to 35 minutes more, or until a meat thermometer inserted in the thickest part of the wings reads 165°F and the wings are crispy. (Note: The wings will likely be done after 45 minutes, but an extra 10 to 15 minutes makes them crispy without drying the meat.)

5. Serve warm with ranch dressing (if using).

Smoked Texas Spicy Drumsticks

Servings: 6

Cooking Time: 60 Minutes

Ingredients:

➢ 8 chicken drumsticks

➢ salt

➢ pepper

➢ 1 Cup Texas Spicy BBQ Sauce

Directions:

1. Pat drumsticks dry with a paper towel and season generously with salt and pepper.

2. Supply your smoker with wood pellets and follow the start-up procedure. Preheat the grill, with the lid closed, to 180° F.

3. Arrange the chicken legs on the grill grate and smoke for 30 minutes. Grill: 180 °F

4. Increase grill temperature to 350°F and cook for an additional 30 minutes. Grill: 350 °F

5. Brush the Texas Spicy BBQ Sauce on each of the drumsticks and cook for an additional 15 to 30 minutes, or until an instant-read meat thermometer inserted into the thickest part of the leg (but not touching bone) reaches 165°F. Enjoy! Grill: 350 °F Probe: 165 °F

Bbq Chicken Wings With Spicy Honey Glaze

Servings: 4

Cooking Time: 30 Minutes

Ingredients:

- 4 Pound chicken wings
- 6 Ounce Chicken Rub
- 2 Tablespoon corn starch
- 1 Cup honey
- 1 Cup Sriracha
- 1/2 Cup soy sauce
- 2 Tablespoon sesame oil
- 3 Tablespoon unsalted butter
- 2 Tablespoon sesame seeds

Directions:

1. Supply your smoker with wood pellets and follow the start-up procedure. Preheat the grill, with the lid closed, to 375° F.

2. While grill is preheating, dry off chicken wings with a paper towel. Mix the Traeger Chicken rub with the cornstarch and coat both sides of the chicken wings.

3. When the grill is heated, place the wings on the grill for 35 minutes flipping half way through. Grill: 375 ˚F

4. While the wings are cooking, mix the honey, Sriracha, soy sauce, sesame seed oil, and unsalted butter and heat on a stove top.

5. After the wings have cooked for 35 minutes, check the temperature. The minimum temperature must reach an internal temperature of 165 degrees F. An internal temperature between 175 to 180 degrees F may yield a better texture. Grill: 375 ˚F Probe: 177 ˚F

6. When wings are done, place in large bowl and toss with the warmed sauce.

7. Place wings on platter and sprinkle the sesame seeds. Enjoy!

Gen's Old-fashioned Barbecued Chicken

Servings: 6

Cooking Time: 90 Minutes

Ingredients:

- 2 whole chickens, each about 4 to 4½lb (1.8 to 2kg)
- 6 tbsp unsalted butter, melted
- seasoned salt
- low-carb barbecue sauce

Directions:

1. Supply your smoker with wood pellets and follow the start-up procedure. Preheat the grill, with the lid closed, to 350° F.

2. Cut each chicken into 8 pieces: 2 wings, 2 breasts, 2 legs, 2 thighs. Rinse under cold running water and pat dry with paper towels. Place on a rimmed sheet pan. Brush with butter and season with seasoned salt.

3. Place the chicken skin side down on the grate and grill for 30 minutes. Turn and continue to grill until the internal temperature in the thickest part of a breast or a thigh reaches 165°F (74°C), about 45 minutes to 1 hour. During the last 10 minutes, brush the chicken with barbecue sauce.

4. Transfer the chicken to a platter. Serve with additional barbecue sauce.

Buffalo Chicken Thighs

Servings: 4

Cooking Time: 15 Minutes

Ingredients:

- ➢ 6 bone-in, skin-on chicken thighs
- ➢ Pork & Poultry Rub
- ➢ 2 Cup Buffalo wing sauce
- ➢ 8 Tablespoon butter
- ➢ blue cheese crumbles, for serving
- ➢ ranch dressing, for serving

Directions:

1. Supply your smoker with wood pellets and follow the start-up procedure. Preheat the grill, with the lid closed, to 450° F.

2. Generously season the chicken thighs with Traeger Pork & Poultry Rub and place directly on the grill grate. Grill: 450 ˚F

3. Cook for 8 to 10 minutes, flipping once. Grill: 450 ˚F

4. In a small saucepan, combine the wing sauce and the butter over medium heat, stirring occasionally.

5. Dip the cooked chicken thighs into the wing sauce and butter mixture, turning to coat both sides evenly. Grill: 450 ˚F Probe: 175 ˚F

6. Return the sauced chicken thighs to the grill and cook for an additional 4 to 5 minutes, or until the internal temperature reads 175°F on an instant-read meat thermometer. Grill: 450 ˚F Probe: 175 ˚F

7. Sprinkle with the blue cheese and drizzle with ranch dressing, if desired. Enjoy!

Lemon & Herb Chicken

Servings: 3-4   Cooking Time: 75 Minutes

Ingredients:

- 1 roaster chicken, about 4lb (1.8kg), preferably organic
- 1 large sweet onion, peeled and sliced lengthwise into 8 wedges
- ½ cup chicken stock or broth
- sprigs of fresh rosemary, thyme, parsley, tarragon, or chives (or a mix)
- lemon wedges
- for the butter
- 4 tbsp unsalted butter, at room temperature
- 1 garlic clove, peeled and finely minced
- 2 tbsp chopped fresh herbs, such as rosemary, thyme, parsley, tarragon, or chives (or a mix)
- 2 tsp lemon zest
- 2 tsp freshly squeezed lemon juice
- ½ tsp coarse salt
- ½ tsp freshly ground black pepper

Directions:

1. Supply your smoker with wood pellets and follow the start-up procedure. Preheat the grill, with the lid closed, to 400° F.

2. In a small bowl, make the herb butter by combining the ingredients.

3. Place the chicken on a rimmed sheet pan and tuck the lemon rinds from the butter into the main cavity. Rub the outside of the chicken with the herb butter. (Reserve any remainder.) Tuck the wings behind the back and tie the legs together with butcher's twine. Place the onion wedges in a shallow roasting pan to help form a natural rack for the chicken. (Alternatively, place several large carrots, trimmed and peeled, on the bottom of the pan.) Place the chicken on the onion rack. Add the chicken stock and any remaining herbed butter and lemon juice.

4. Place the roasting pan on the grate, roast the chicken for 30 minutes, and then baste with the juices from the bottom of the pan. Baste every 15 minutes until the chicken is golden brown and the internal temperature reaches 165°F (74°C), about 45 minutes more.

5. Transfer the chicken to a cutting board and let rest for 10 minutes. Carve the chicken and place the slices on a platter with a deep well. Spoon some of the juices over the chicken. Scatter fresh herbs over the top. Serve with the lemon wedges.

Buffalo Chicken

Servings: 6	Cooking Time: 90 Minutes

Ingredients:

- 1 1/2 Tbsp Apple Cider Vinegar
- 3 Tbsp Bleu Cheese, Crumbled
- 1/4 Cup Buffalo Sauce
- 1/2 Cup Butter, Unsalted, Cubed
- 1/4 Tsp Cayenne Pepper
- 3 Celery Stalks, Cut Into Sticks
- 1 Cup Cheddar Jack Cheese, Shredded
- 1 Lb Chicken Breast, Boneless, Skinless
- 3 Oz Cream Cheese, Softened
- 1/8 Tsp Garlic, Granulated
- 2/3 Cup Hot Pepper Sauce
- 12 Jalapeno Peppers
- Mason Jar(S)
- 1/4 Red Bell Pepper, Chopped
- 2 Scallions, Sliced Thin
- Shredded Chicken
- 3 Tbsp Sour Cream
- To Taste, Sweet Heat Rub
- 1/2 Tsp Sweet Heat Rub (For Sauce)
- 1/4 Tsp Worcestershire Sauce

Directions:

1. Supply your smoker with wood pellets and follow the start-up procedure. Preheat the grill, with the lid open, to 200° F. If using a gas or charcoal grill, set it up for low, indirect heat.

2. Season chicken breasts with Sweet Heat, then place on the grill. Smoke for 1 hour, then remove from the grill, and set aside to rest.

3. While the chicken is resting, prepare the Buffalo sauce: Set a small cast iron pan or saucepan on the grill. Open the sear slide and increase the grill temperature to 350° F. Add the hot pepper sauce, apple cider vinegar, Worcestershire sauce, Sweet Heat, cayenne, and granulated garlic to the skillet, and whisk to combine. When the sauce begins to bubble, remove the skillet from the grill and whisk in butter. Transfer the sauce to a mason jar.

4. Shred the chicken with 2 forks in the sauce skillet. Set aside.

5. Prepare the filling: In a mixing bowl, use a hand mixer to blend cream cheese, bleu cheese, Buffalo sauce and sour cream. Fold in scallions, red bell pepper, and shredded chicken.

6. Prepare the peppers: Cut each jalapeño in half, lengthwise. Use a paring knife or teaspoon to scrape out the seeds and membrane, then place in a cast iron skillet (might need to divide between 2 skillets). Stuff the mixture into the jalapeño halves, then top with shredded cheese.

7. Transfer peppers to the grill, with the sear slide closed. Close the lid and cook for 15 to 20 minutes, until peppers begin to soften and cheese has melted.

8. Remove the peppers from the grill, transfer to a serving board or platter, and serve warm with extra Buffalo sauce.

BEEF LAMB AND GAME RECIPES

Delicious Barbecue Beef Brisket

Servings: 12

Cooking Time: 480 Minutes

Ingredients:

➢ 1 Beef Soup, Campbells Can

➢ 1 - 12 To 14 Lb Packer Beef, Brisket

Directions:

1. The night before you plan on cooking the brisket, trim the surface fat off the brisket with your sharp boning knife. Trim to leave about 1/8 to ¼ in fat.

2. Place the brisket in an unscented trash bag or on a sheet pan fat side up and season the meat side liberally with your favorite Rub. Let rest on the counter for 30 minutes until the rub is all soaked up. Flip the brisket over and season the fat side liberally. Cover or wrap up the brisket and put in the fridge overnight.

3. Prep your Grill by cleaning the grates, grease tray and firepot is clean. Supply your smoker with wood pellets and follow the start-up procedure. Preheat the grill, with the lid closed, to 250° F.

4. When grill has settled to 250°F place brisket in center of grill fat side down and cook for 4 hours.

5. After 4 hours, insert the meat probe into the fat seam between the point and flat so the end of the meat probe is in the center of the fat seam and continue to cook for about 2 more hours.

6. Prep aluminum foil to wrap the brisket in by tearing off 4 sheets of foil at least twice as large as the brisket. Plus one more piece about the same size as the brisket.

7. When the meat thermometer reads 150°F to 160°F wrap the brisket in foil by placing the brisket fat side down on 2 sheets of foil. The cover with the other 2 sheets of foil and tightly roll/fold 3 sides up to seal – leaving one side open. Leave the meat probe in place in the brisket and lay the probe wire between the bottom and top foil sheets. Roll/fold the meat probe wire between the foil sheets as you are closing the foil. Dump the can of Campbell's Beef Consume into the foil through the open end and roll/fold that end closed.

8. Place the small foil sheet on the grill grate and place the foil-wrapped brisket on the small foil sheet on the grate. The small foil sheet will prevent the foil from sticking to the grate to prevent the foil from ripping and losing the foil juice that you can use later.

9.   Continue to cook until the meat thermometer reads 200°F. Then unwrap one or two sides of the foil being careful not to lose any of the liquid in the foil. Insert a dinner fork into the flat portion of the brisket – if it goes in and out like a hot knife through butter it is done, if it has very much resistance, seal the sides of the foil and place back in grill and cook until the meat thermometer reads 205°F and test for tenderness again.

10. When the brisket is done, remove from grill, wrap in a clean towel and place in a small clean cooler to rest for at least 2 hours.

11. When ready to slice, remove brisket from foil. Separate the point end from the flat end by running your slicing knife down the fat seam. Slice the brisket across the grain into slices just thick enough to hold together.

12. Cube the point section into ½ in sq cubes by slicing ½ in slices across the grain first and then ½ in slices with the grain.

13. Place all slices and cubes into a pan and pour some of the liquid from the foil over the brisket.

14. Serve with your favorite BBQ Sauce on the side.

Flavour Smoked Chuck Roast

Servings: 6

Cooking Time: 540 Minutes

Ingredients:

➢ 3 cups beef stock, divided

➢ 1, 3 lb chuck roast

➢ 3 tbsp sweet heat rub

➢ 1 yellow onion

Directions:

1. Place chuck roast in a 9x13 baking pan. Sprinkle generously with   Sweet Heat Rub and rub to coat evenly on all sides.

2. Cover pan with foil and refrigerate overnight.

3. The next day, remove chuck roast from refrigerator and let it come to room temperature.

4. Supply your smoker with wood pellets and follow the start-up procedure. Preheat the grill, with the lid closed, to 225° F. If using a gas or charcoal grill, set it for low heat.

5. Insert a temperature probe into the thickest side of the roast, then place chuck roast directly on grill grate. Close lid and smoke for 3 hours.

6. Spray roast with 1 cup of beef stock every hour.

7. Slice the onion and place in a 9x13 aluminum pan. Pour the remaining cup of stock over the onions and set roast on top of onions.

8. Increase temperature to 250°F and cook an additional 2 ½ to 3 hours, or until internal temperature reaches 165°F.

9. Once 165°F internal temperature is reached, cover roast with aluminum foil, and cook another 2 ½ to 3 hours, or until internal temperature reaches 200°F.

10. Remove chuck roast from grill.

11. Allow roast to rest 15 minutes, then remove from pan and shred with meat claws. For added moistness and flavor, pour some remaining cooking stock over the shredded roast and serve.

Baked Ziti With Italian Sausage

Servings: 6

Cooking Time: 20 Minutes

Ingredients:

- 1 Pound Ziti, cooked 1 minute less than directions, and dried
- 1 Jar Spaghetti Sauce
- 1 Teaspoon garlic, minced
- 1 Pinch red pepper flakes
- 1 Pound Italian Sausage, cooked
- salt and pepper
- 2 Cup Mozzarella Cheese, Grated
- 1/4 Cup Parmesan cheese

Directions:

1. Supply your smoker with wood pellets and follow the start-up procedure. Preheat the grill, with the lid closed, to 450° F.

2. In a large bowl, pour your spaghetti sauce over the cooked pasta, add garlic, red pepper flakes, and salt and pepper to taste. Toss. Fold the sausage into the pasta mixture.

3. Coat a 9 x 13 x 2-inch baking dish with nonstick cooking spray.

4. Pour half of the pasta mixture into your prepared baking dish. Sprinkle with half of the mozzarella. Pour remaining pasta into the dish, smooth out the top and add the remaining mozzarella.

5. Bake in Traeger until cheese is golden brown and bubbly, about 20 minutes.

6. Remove and sprinkle with parmesan cheese. Enjoy!

Beef Chuck Ribs

Servings: 4

Cooking Time: 300 Minutes

Ingredients:

- ½ cup yellow or Dijon mustard
- 2 tbsp Worcestershire sauce
- 8 bone-in beef chuck ribs, about 2 to 2½lb (1 to 1.2kg) total coarse salt
- fresh coarsely ground black pepper
- steak sauce or Horseradish Sauce
- for the mop sauce
- 1 cup low-carb beer or sugar-free dark-colored soda
- ½ cup cold brewed coffee
- 2 tbsp light soy sauce or liquid aminos
- 2 tbsp unsalted butter, melted

Directions:

1. Supply your smoker with wood pellets and follow the start-up procedure. Preheat the grill, with the lid closed, to 250° F.

2. In a food-safe spray bottle, make the mop sauce by combining the ingredients. Set aside.

3. In a small bowl, combine the mustard and Worcestershire sauce. Lightly brush the mixture on the meaty sides of the short ribs. Season with salt and pepper.

4. Place the ribs bone side down on the grate and smoke until the internal temperature reaches 200°F (93°C), about 4 to 5 hours. Occasionally spritz the meat with the mop sauce after the first hour—about every 30 minutes.

5. Transfer the short ribs to a platter. Serve with steak sauce.

Baked Maple Venison Sausage Quiche

Servings: 4

Cooking Time: 45 Minutes

Ingredients:

- 2 Pound Venison, ground
- 12 Whole egg
- 16 Ounce Cottage Cheese, fat free
- 1 1/2 Cup Cheese, Colby/Cheddar
- 1 Teaspoon baking powder
- 1 Whole white onion, chopped
- 4 Ounce Green Chiles, canned, chopped

Directions:

1. Cook ground venison in a medium sauté pan over medium high until browned. Drain off excess fat and set venison aside.

2. Whisk eggs in a large mixing bowl. Add remaining ingredients, stirring after each addition. Transfer mixture to one 13x9 pan and one 9x9 pan.

3. Supply your smoker with wood pellets and follow the start-up procedure. Preheat the grill, with the lid closed, to 350° F.

4. Place casserole dish directly on grill grate and cook for 45 minutes or until a knife inserted into the center comes out clean. Let cool 10 minutes before serving. Enjoy!

5. This recipe was provided by Pro Team member Josh and Sarah Bowmar. Access this, and over a thousand other Traeger recipes on the Traeger App.

Reverse-seared Elk Tenderloin With Green Peppercorn Sauce

Servings: 8   Cooking Time: 66 Minutes

Ingredients:

- 1 whole elk tenderloin, about 2½lb (1.2kg)
- extra virgin olive oil
- coarse salt
- fresh coarsely ground black pepper
- granulated garlic
- for the sauce
- 3 tbsp unsalted butter, divided
- 2 large shallots, peeled and finely diced
- 2 cups low-salt beef stock
- ½ cup Cognac or brandy
- 1 cup heavy whipping cream
- 1 tbsp Dijon mustard
- ¼ brined green peppercorns, drained
- 2 tbsp fresh coarsely ground dried green peppercorns
- coarse salt
- freshly ground black pepper

Directions:

1. Supply your smoker with wood pellets and follow the start-up procedure. Preheat the grill, with the lid closed, to 225° F.

2. Tie the tenderloin at 2-inch (5cm) intervals with butcher's twine. Tuck the tail under the thicker portion of the tenderloin and secure with twine. Trim any loose strings close to the knots. Place the tenderloin on a rimmed sheet pan and use your hands to coat all the sides with olive oil. Generously season with salt and pepper and granulated garlic.

3. In a skillet on the stovetop over medium heat, make the sauce by melting 2 tablespoons of butter. Add the shallots and cook until softened but not browned, about 2 to 3 minutes. Add the beef stock and raise the heat to medium high. Bring the mixture to a boil and reduce to ½ cup, about 10 minutes. Add the Cognac and cream and then whisk in the mustard.

4. Crush some of the brined peppercorns with the side of a knife. Stir all the brined and dried peppercorns into the sauce. Cook until the sauce is thick enough to coat a spoon, about 3 minutes. Whisk in the remaining 1 tablespoon of butter. Season with salt and pepper to taste. Keep warm.

5. Place the tenderloin on the grate at an angle to the bars. Smoke until the internal temperature in the thickest part of the meat reaches 110 to 115°F (43 to 46°C), about 1 hour. Transfer the tenderloin to a rimmed sheet pan lined with aluminum foil.

6. Raise the temperature to 500°F (260°C). Place the tenderloin on the grate at an angle to the bars. Sear until the internal temperature reaches 135°F (57°C), about 2 to 3 minutes per side.

7. Transfer the meat to a cutting board. Remove the butcher's twine and slice the tenderloin into steaks. Place the slices on a platter. Rewarm and rewhisk the sauce if necessary. Spoon over the steaks before serving.

Flavour Texas Twinkies

Servings: 7-14

Cooking Time: 40 Minutes

Ingredients:

- 14, slices bacon
- ½ cup BBQ sauce
- 1 lb. brisket
- 8 oz. cream cheese
- 1 tsp cumin
- 14 large jalapeños
- ½ tsp pepper
- 1 cup pepper jack cheese, grated
- 2 tsp hickory bacon rub
- ½ tsp salt

Directions:

1. Supply your smoker with wood pellets and follow the start-up procedure. Preheat the grill, with the lid closed, to 400° F. If using a gas or charcoal grill, set it for medium-high heat.

2. In a food processor, combine the brisket, Hickory Bacon, cumin, salt, pepper, pepper jack and cream cheese. Pulse several times until well combined. Transfer to a bowl and place into refrigerator to chill while preparing jalapeños.

3. Place jalapeños on a sheet tray. Cut each in half lengthwise and remove the seeds and rib with a spoon or by hand, then discard. Note: we recommend using gloves when handling jalapenos, as the seeds can be very hot.

4. Fill each jalapeño half with cream cheese mixture until full, then place other jalapeño half on top. Wrap each jalapeño with a slice of bacon, then skewer crosswise with toothpicks.

5. Place a mesh, metal pan on grill grate and transfer jalapeños to pan. Cover grill and cook for 35 minutes.

6. Open grill and baste jalapeños generously with BBQ sauce, close grill and continue to cook another 5 minutes.

7. Remove from grill and serve hot.

Chorizo Cheese Stuffed Burgers

Servings: 2

Cooking Time: 45 Minutes

Ingredients:

- 2 Pound ground beef, 80% lean
- 4 Ounce Prime Rib Rub
- 12 Ounce Chorizo
- 2 Slices cheddar cheese
- 4 Whole Brioche Bun
- Tomatoes, sliced
- red onion, sliced
- lettuce, sliced

Directions:

1. Mix 2 lb of 80/20 ground beef in mixing bowl with Traeger Prime Rib Rub.

2. Divide the ground beef into eight 1/4 lb patties. Make one patty the base, lay down 1/4 of a cheese slice, add 3 oz. of chorizo and top with another 1/4 cheese slice. Apply another patty on top and pinch the ends all the way around the burger to seal together the two patties.

3. Repeat until all 4 patties are done.

4. Supply your smoker with wood pellets and follow the start-up procedure. Preheat the grill, with the lid closed, to 325° F.

5. Place burgers on the Traeger for 15 minutes on each side. If desired, top each burger with slice of Cheddar cheese, let melt. Remove from Traeger and let rest for 10 minutes tented with foil.

6. While burgers are resting, brush the brioche buns with melted better and toast for 30-45 seconds on the grill.

7. Remove buns from grill and assemble burger with toppings. Enjoy!

Spiced Smoked Kielbasa Dogs

Ingredients:

- 1 tsp all spice, ground
- 2 tsp black peppercorns, ground
- 3 tbsp brown sugar
- 1 cup distilled ice water, divided
- 1 1/2 tsp garlic powder
- 1 1/2 lbs ground beef

- 5 lbs ground pork
- 32 - 35 hog casings
- 2 tbsp kosher salt
- 2 tsp marjoram, dried
- 1 1/2 tsp paprika
- 1 1/4 tsp speed cure, pink salt curing

Directions:

1. In a glass bowl or measuring cup, cover hog casings in warm water and let soak for 1 hour.

2. In a small bowl, whisk together brown sugar, salt, black pepper, marjoram, garlic powder, paprika, allspice, and speed cure.

3. In a large tub, combine ground pork and ground beef. Mix together by hand, then add seasoning and distilled ice water. Mix mixture by hand for 1 minute, until seasoning is incorporated throughout.

4. Prepare the sausage stuffer, and fit one hog casing over a 1 to 1 ¼ inch horn. Place a sheet tray, with a bit of water on it, underneath the nozzle of the stuffer and start filling the casings.

5. Once the casings are filled, twist off into desired lengths, and refrigerate overnight.

6. Hang the links with S-hooks from the top rack of your Grill or Smoker. Smoke on SMOKE mode for 3 hours. Supply your smoker with wood pellets and follow the start-up procedure. Preheat the grill, with the lid closed, to 300° F, which will raise the temperature of the smoking cabinet to 170°F. If using a vertical smoker, keep smoking on SMOKE mode. Continue smoking the sausage for another 1 to 2 hours, until the internal temperature of the sausage reaches 155° F.

7. Remove sausage from the smoking cabinet and either enjoy hot with your favorite toppings, or place in an ice water bath for 15 minutes, dry at room temperature and refrigerate or freeze for future use.

Sweetheart Steak With Lobster Ceviche

Servings: 2

Cooking Time: 15 Minutes

Ingredients:

- 1 (20 Oz) Boneless Strip Steak Or Rib Steak, Butterflied Into Heart Shape
- 2 Teaspoon Jacobsen Salt Co. Pure Kosher Sea Salt
- 2 Teaspoon black pepper
- 2 Tablespoon Raw Dark Chocolate, finely chopped
- 1/2 Tablespoon olive oil
- 1 1/2 Pound Lobster Tail
- 1 Cup lemon juice
- 1/3 Cup lime juice
- 1/2 jalapeño, diced

Directions:

1. For the Sweetheart Steak, draw a large heart on a piece of cardboard, shape to size of meat selected. Cut out cardboard heart shape, then trim meat into heart shape.

2. Combine Jacobsen Salt, pepper, chocolate, and olive oil in a small bowl. Place on top of cut steak.

3. Cut raw lobster tail, remove meat, and chop. In a separate medium bowl, combine the lemon juice, lime juice, and jalapeno.

4. Toss in the lobster meat; ensure it is completely submerged in the liquid. Let lobster soak for 30 minutes. The citric acid actually cooks the lobster meat. If you prefer to have fully-cooked meat, grill lobster in shell for 3-5 minutes at 350 degrees F. Grill: 350 °F

5. Remove from grill, then toss with lemon juice, lime juice, and jalapeno.

6. Supply your smoker with wood pellets and follow the start-up procedure. Preheat the grill, with the lid closed, to 450° F.

7. Place the steak directly on the grill grate and cook for 5 to 7 minutes per side, or until you've reached desired doneness. Remove from grill. Let rest for 5 minutes. Grill: 450 °F

8. Serve lobster ceviche over steak. Enjoy!

Reverse Seared Rib-eye Caps

Servings: 4

Cooking Time: 45 Minutes

Ingredients:

- ➢ 1 1/2 Pound rib-eye cap
- ➢ 2 Tablespoon Coffee Rub
- ➢ 2 Tablespoon Beef Rub

Directions:

1. Trim the rib-eye cap of excess silverskin and fat, if needed. Cut the cap into 4 equal portions and roll into steaks. Tie with butcher's twine to secure.

2. In a small bowl, combine both rubs. Season the steaks liberally with the rub mixture and set aside while the grill heats up.

3. Supply your smoker with wood pellets and follow the start-up procedure. Preheat the grill, with the lid closed, to 225° F.

4. Place the steaks directly on the grill grate, and smoke for 30 to 45 minutes until the internal temperature reaches 120°F. Grill: 225 °F Probe: 120 °F

5. Remove from the grill and set aside to rest.

6. Increase the grill temperature to 450°F. Grill: 450 °F

7. Place the steaks directly on the grill grate and cook 3 to 4 minutes per side, or until the internal temperature reaches 130°F. Grill: 450 °F Probe: 130 °F

8. Remove from grill and let rest 5 minutes before serving. Enjoy!

3-2-1 Bbq Beef Cheeks

Servings: 8

Cooking Time: 480 Minutes

Ingredients:

- 2 (2 lb) beef cheeks, silverskin trimmed
- Beef Rub
- 1/4 Cup liquid of choice (beef stock, dark beer, etc.)
- 2 Tablespoon honey, brown sugar or other sweetener

Directions:

1. Make sure the beef cheeks are trimmed of all silverskin. Season liberally with Traeger Beef rub.
2. Supply your smoker with wood pellets and follow the start-up procedure. Preheat the grill, with the lid closed, to 180° F.
3. Place beef cheeks directly on the grill grate and cook until they reach an internal temperature of 165°F, about 3 hours. Remove from grill and place the cheeks in a small rimmed baking dish. Grill: 180 °F Probe: 165 °F
4. Increase grill temperature to 225°F.
5. In a small bowl, combine liquid and sweetener and stir until sweetener is dissolved. Pour mixture into the baking dish and return the cheeks to the grill to cook for an additional two hours. Grill: 225 °F
6. Remove cheeks from the grill and cover with foil. Return to the grill to cook for an additional hour or until the internal temperature reaches 205°F. Grill: 225 °F Probe: 205 °F
7. Remove from the grill and allow the steam to escape. Wrap with foil again and let rest for 30 minutes before shredding or slicing. Enjoy!

Spiced Leg Of Lamb Gyros

Servings: 8 – 10   Cooking Time: 180 Minutes

Ingredients:

- 1 Tbsp Black Pepper
- 4 Oz. Cremini Mushrooms
- ¼ Cup Dijon Mustard
- 8, Smashed Garlic Cloves
- 1 Cup + 1 Tbsp Grapeseed Oil, Divided
- 5 Lb, Bone-In Sirloin Leg Of Lamb
- ⅓ Cup Lemon Juice
- ½ Tbsp + 1 Tsp Dried, Divided Oregano
- 8-10 Pita
- Large Wedge Chop Red Onion
- 1 Tbsp Rosemary Leaves, Dried
- ⅔ Cup Scallions, Chopped
- 3 Tbsp, Coarse Sea Salt
- ½ Tbsp Thyme, Dried
- Tzatziki Sauce
- 1 Vine-Ripe Tomato, Chopped

Directions:

1. Fire up your grill and preheat to "Smoke" mode. If using a gas or charcoal grill, set it up for low, indirect heat.

2. In a food processor, combine grapeseed oil, lemon juice, mustard, scallions, garlic, rosemary, thyme, salt and pepper. Process until it forms a thick marinade.

3. Score the fat cap of the lamb, then truss with butcher's twine. Pour two-thirds of the marinade onto the leg of lamb to cover completely. Set remaining marinade aside for vegetables. Wrap the lamb in foil and marinate at room temperature for 1 hour.

4. Place the lamb in the smoking cabinet by hanging truss from S hooks. Insert temperature probe and smoke for 45 minutes. Increase the temperature to 400°F.

5. Supply your smoker with wood pellets and follow the start-up procedure. Preheat the grill, with the lid closed, to 225 to 250° F. (If you're using a grill or vertical smoker, set your temperature to 225°F). Once it has reached this temperature, make sure the upper chimney caps are fully open, and you can lower the grill temp to 300°F. As long as the cabinet doors remain closed this should maintain temperature in the upper cabinet.

6. Smoke the lamb until the internal temperature of the meat reaches 135°F, about 3 hours.

7. While the lamb is cooking, skewer together red onion and mushrooms. Brush with remaining marinade, then transfer to grill with sear slide open, 3 to 5 minutes. In a small bowl combine 1 tbsp of grape seed oil and 1 tsp of oregano and brush lightly over pita breads. Grill pita bread to warm while skewers are on the grill.

8. Remove the leg of lamb from the smoker and loosely cover with aluminum foil. Rest the meat for 30 minutes before slicing.

9. Thinly slice the lamb, and serve in warm pita with grilled mushrooms and onions, and chopped tomatoes, and tzatziki, if desired.

APPETIZERS AND SNACKS

Cold-smoked Cheese

Servings: 6	Cooking Time: 180 Minutes

Ingredients:

- 2lb (1kg) well-chilled hard or semi-hard cheese, such as:
- Edam
- Gouda
- Cheddar
- Monterey Jack
- pepper Jack
- goat cheese
- fresh mozzarella
- Muenster
- aged Parmigiano-Reggiano
- Gruyère
- blue cheese

Directions:

1. Unwrap the cheese and remove any protective wax or coating. Cut into 4-ounce (110g) portions to increase the surface area.

2. If possible, move your smoker to a shady area. Place 1 resealable plastic bag filled with ice on top of the drip pan. This is especially important on a warm day because you want to keep the interior temperature of the grill between 70 and 90°F (21 and 32°C) or below.

3. Place a grill mat on one side of the grate. Place the cheese on the mat and allow space between each piece.

4. Fill your smoking tube or pellet maze (see Cast Iron Skillets and Grill Pans) with pellets or sawdust and light according to the manufacturer's instructions. Place the smoking tube on the grate near—but not on—the grill mat. When the tube is smoking consistently, close the grill lid.

5. Smoke the cheese for 1 to 3 hours, replacing the pellets or sawdust and ice if necessary. Monitor the temperature and make sure the cheese isn't beginning to melt. Carefully lift the mat with the cheese to a rimmed baking sheet and let the cheese cool completely before handling.

6. Package the smoked cheese in cheese storage paper or bags or vacuum-seal the cheese, labeling each. (While you can wrap the cheese tightly in plastic wrap, the cheese will spoil faster.) Let the cheese rest for at least 2 to 3 days before eating. It will be even better after 2 weeks.

Pig Pops (sweet-hot Bacon On A Stick)

Servings: 24

Cooking Time: 30 Minutes

Ingredients:

- ➢ Nonstick cooking spray, oil, or butter, for greasing
- ➢ 2 pounds thick-cut bacon (24 slices)
- ➢ 24 metal skewers
- ➢ 1 cup packed light brown sugar
- ➢ 2 to 3 teaspoons cayenne pepper
- ➢ ½ cup maple syrup, divided

Directions:

1. Supply your smoker with wood pellets and follow the start-up procedure. Preheat, with the lid closed, to 350°F.

2. Coat a disposable aluminum foil baking sheet with cooking spray, oil, or butter.

3. Thread each bacon slice onto a metal skewer and place on the prepared baking sheet.

4. In a medium bowl, stir together the brown sugar and cayenne.

5. Baste the top sides of the bacon with ¼ cup of maple syrup.

6. Sprinkle half of the brown sugar mixture over the bacon.

7. Place the baking sheet on the grill, close the lid, and smoke for 15 to 30 minutes.

8. Using tongs, flip the bacon skewers. Baste with the remaining ¼ cup of maple syrup and top with the remaining brown sugar mixture.

9. Continue smoking with the lid closed for 10 to 15 minutes, or until crispy. You can eyeball the bacon and smoke to your desired doneness, but the actual ideal internal temperature for bacon is 155°F

10. Using tongs, carefully remove the bacon skewers from the grill. Let cool completely before handling.

Bacon Pork Pinwheels (kansas Lollipops)

Servings: 4-6

Cooking Time: 20 Minutes

Ingredients:

- 1 Whole Pork Loin, boneless
- To Taste salt and pepper
- To Taste Greek Seasoning
- 4 Slices bacon
- To Taste The Ultimate BBQ Sauce

Directions:

1. When ready to cook, start the smoker and set temperature to 500F. Preheat, lid closed, for 10 to 15 minutes.

2. Trim pork loin of any unwanted silver skin or fat. Using a sharp knife, cut pork loin length wise, into 4 long strips.

3. Lay pork flat, then season with salt, pepper and Cavender's Greek Seasoning.

4. Flip the pork strips over and layer bacon on unseasoned side. Begin tightly rolling the pork strips, with bacon being rolled up on the inside.

5. Secure a skewer all the way through each pork roll to secure it in place. Set the pork rolls down on grill and cook for 15 minutes.

6. Brush BBQ Sauce over the pork. Turn each skewer over, then coat the other side. Let pork cook for another 5-10 minutes, depending on thickness of your pork. Enjoy!

Grilled Guacamole

Servings: 6

Cooking Time: 30 Minutes

Ingredients:

- 3 large avocados, halved and pitted
- 1 lime, halved
- ½ jalapeño, deseeded and deveined
- ½ small white or red onion, peeled
- 2 garlic cloves, peeled and skewered on a toothpick
- 1 tsp coarse salt, plus more
- 1½ tbsp reduced-fat mayo
- 2 tbsp chopped fresh cilantro
- 2 tbsp crumbled queso fresco (optional)
- tortilla chips

Directions:

1. Supply your smoker with wood pellets and follow the start-up procedure. Preheat the grill, with the lid closed, to 225° F.

2. Place the avocados, lime, jalapeño, and onion cut sides down on the grate. Use the toothpicks to balance the garlic cloves between the bars. Smoke for 30 minutes. (You want the vegetables to retain most of their rawness.)

3. Transfer everything to a cutting board. Remove the garlic cloves from the toothpick and roughly chop. Sprinkle with the salt and continue to mince the garlic until it begins to form a paste. Scrape the garlic and salt into a large bowl.

4. Scoop the avocado flesh from the peels into the bowl. Squeeze the juice of ½ lime over the avocado. Mash the avocados but leave them somewhat chunky. Finely dice the jalapeño. Dice 2 tablespoons of onion. (Reserve the remaining onion for another use.) Add the jalapeño, onion, mayo, and cilantro to the bowl. Stir gently to combine. Taste for seasoning, adding more salt, lime juice, and jalapeño as desired.

5. Transfer the guacamole to a serving bowl. Top with the queso fresco (if using). Serve with tortilla chips.

Pigs In A Blanket

Servings: 4-6

Cooking Time: 15 Minutes

Ingredients:

- 2 Tablespoon Poppy Seeds
- 1 Tablespoon Dried Minced Onion
- 2 Teaspoon garlic, minced
- 2 Tablespoon Sesame Seeds
- 1 Teaspoon salt
- 8 Ounce Original Crescent Dough
- 1/4 Cup Dijon mustard
- 1 Large egg, beaten

Directions:

1. When ready to cook, start your smoker at 350 degrees F, and preheat with lid closed, 10 to 15 minutes.
2. Mix together poppy seeds, dried minced onion, dried minced garlic, salt and sesame seeds. Set aside.
3. Cut each triangle of crescent roll dough into thirds lengthwise, making 3 small strips from each roll.
4. Brush the dough strips lightly with Dijon mustard. Put the mini hot dogs on 1 end of the dough and roll up.
5. Arrange them, seam side down, on a greased baking pan. Brush with egg wash and sprinkle with seasoning mixture.
6. Bake in smoker until golden brown, about 12 to 15 minutes.
7. Serve with mustard or dipping sauce of your choice. Enjoy!

Bacon-wrapped Jalapeño Poppers

Servings: 12

Cooking Time: 30 Minutes

Ingredients:

- 8 ounces cream cheese, softened
- ½ cup shredded Cheddar cheese
- ¼ cup chopped scallions
- 1 teaspoon chipotle chile powder or regular chili powder
- 1 teaspoon garlic powder
- 1 teaspoon salt
- 18 large jalapeño peppers, stemmed, seeded, and halved lengthwise
- 1 pound bacon (precooked works well)

Directions:

1. Supply your smoker with wood pellets and follow the start-up procedure. Preheat, with the lid closed, to 350°F. Line a baking sheet with aluminum foil.

2. In a small bowl, combine the cream cheese, Cheddar cheese, scallions, chipotle powder, garlic powder, and salt.

3. Stuff the jalapeño halves with the cheese mixture.

4. Cut the bacon into pieces big enough to wrap around the stuffed pepper halves.

5. Wrap the bacon around the peppers and place on the prepared baking sheet.

6. Put the baking sheet on the grill grate, close the lid, and smoke the peppers for 30 minutes, or until the cheese is melted and the bacon is cooked through and crisp.

7. Let the jalapeño poppers cool for 3 to 5 minutes. Serve warm.

Chuckwagon Beef Jerky

Servings: 6

Cooking Time: 300 Minutes

Ingredients:

- 2½lb (1.2kg) boneless top or bottom round steak, sirloin tip, flank steak, or venison
- 1 cup sugar-free dark-colored soda
- 1 cup cold brewed coffee
- ½ cup light soy sauce
- ¼ cup Worcestershire sauce

- 2 tbsp whiskey (optional)
- 2 tsp chili powder
- 1½ tsp garlic salt
- 1 tsp onion powder
- 1 tsp pink curing salt

Directions:

1. Slice the meat into ¼-inch-thick (.5cm) strips, trimming off any visible fat or gristle. (Slice against the grain for more tender jerky and with the grain for chewier jerky.) Place the meat in a large resealable plastic bag.

2. In a small bowl, whisk together the soda, coffee, soy sauce, Worcestershire sauce, whiskey (if using), chili powder, garlic salt, onion powder, and curing salt (if using). Whisk until the salt dissolves. Pour the mixture over the meat and reseal the bag. Refrigerate for 24 to 48 hours, turning the bag several times to redistribute the brine.

3. Supply your smoker with wood pellets and follow the start-up procedure. Preheat the grill, with the lid closed, to 150° F.

4. Drain the meat and discard the brine. Place the strips of meat in a single layer on paper towels and blot any excess moisture.

5. Place the meat in a single layer on the grate and smoke for 4 to 5 hours, turning once or twice. (If you're aware of hot spots on your grate, rotate the strips so they smoke evenly.) To test for doneness, bend one or two pieces in the middle. They should be dry but still somewhat pliant. Or simply eat a piece to see if it's done to your liking.

6. For the best texture, when you remove the meat from the grill, place the still-warm jerky in a resealable plastic bag and let rest for 30 minutes. (You might see condensation form on the inside of the bag, but the moisture will be reabsorbed by the meat.) Or let the meat cool completely and then store in a resealable plastic bag or covered container. The jerky will last a few days at room temperature but will last longer (up to 2 weeks) if refrigerated.

Pulled Pork Loaded Nachos

Servings: 4	Cooking Time: 10 Minutes

Ingredients:

- 2 cups leftover smoked pulled pork
- 1 small sweet onion, diced
- 1 medium tomato, diced
- 1 jalapeño pepper, seeded and diced
- 1 garlic clove, minced
- 1 teaspoon salt
- 1 teaspoon freshly ground black pepper
- 1 bag tortilla chips
- 1 cup shredded Cheddar cheese
- ½ cup The Ultimate BBQ Sauce, divided
- ½ cup shredded jalapeño Monterey Jack cheese
- Juice of ½ lime
- 1 avocado, halved, pitted, and sliced
- 2 tablespoons sour cream
- 1 tablespoon chopped fresh cilantro

Directions:

1. Supply your smoker with wood pellets and follow the start-up procedure. Preheat, with the lid closed, to 375°F.

2. Heat the pulled pork in the microwave.

3. In a medium bowl, combine the onion, tomato, jalapeño, garlic, salt, and pepper, and set aside.

4. Arrange half of the tortilla chips in a large cast iron skillet. Spread half of the warmed pork on top and cover with the Cheddar cheese. Top with half of the onion-jalapeño mixture, then drizzle with ¼ cup of barbecue sauce.

5. Layer on the remaining tortilla chips, then the remaining pork and the Monterey Jack cheese. Top with the remaining onion-jalapeño mixture and drizzle with the remaining ¼ cup of barbecue sauce.

6. Place the skillet on the grill, close the lid, and smoke for about 10 minutes, or until the cheese is melted and bubbly. (Watch to make sure your chips don't burn!)

7. Squeeze the lime juice over the nachos, top with the avocado slices and sour cream, and garnish with the cilantro before serving hot.

Smoked Turkey Sandwich

Servings: 1

Cooking Time: 15 Minutes

Ingredients:

- 2 slices sourdough bread
- 2 tablespoons butter, at room temperature
- 2 (1-ounce) slices Swiss cheese
- 4 ounces leftover Smoked Turkey
- 1 teaspoon garlic salt

Directions:

1. Supply your smoker with wood pellets and follow the start-up procedure. Preheat the grill, with the lid closed, to 375°F.

2. Coat one side of each bread slice with 1 tablespoon of butter and sprinkle the buttered sides with garlic salt.

3. Place 1 slice of cheese on each unbuttered side of the bread, and then put the turkey on the cheese.

4. Close the sandwich, buttered sides out, and place it directly on the grill grate. Cook for 5 minutes. Flip the sandwich and cook for 5 minutes more. Remove the sandwich from the grill, cut it in half, and serve.

Deviled Eggs With Smoked Paprika

Servings: 6   Cooking Time: 30 Minutes

Ingredients:

- 6 large eggs
- 3 tbsp reduced-fat mayo, plus more
- 1 tsp Dijon or yellow mustard
- ½ tsp Spanish smoked paprika or regular paprika, plus more
- dash of hot sauce
- coarse salt
- freshly ground black pepper
- for garnishing
- small sprigs of fresh parsley, dill, tarragon, or cilantro
- chopped chives
- minced scallions
- Mustard Caviar
- sliced green or black olives
- celery leaves
- sliced radishes
- diced bell peppers
- sliced cherry tomatoes
- fresh or pickled jalapeños
- sliced or diced pickles
- slivers of sun-dried tomatoes
- bacon crumbles
- smoked salmon
- Hawaiian black salt
- Caviar

Directions:

1. Supply your smoker with wood pellets and follow the start-up procedure. Preheat the grill, with the lid closed, to 180° F.

2. On the stovetop over medium-high heat, bring a saucepan of water to a boil. (Make sure there's enough water in the saucepan to cover the eggs by 1 inch [5cm].) Use a slotted spoon to gently lower the eggs into the water. Lower the heat to maintain a simmer. Set a timer for 13 minutes.

3. Prepare an ice bath by combining ice and cold water in a large bowl. Carefully transfer the eggs to the ice bath when the timer goes off.

4. When the eggs are cool enough to handle, gently tap them all over to crack the shell. Carefully peel the eggs. Rinse under cold running water to remove any clinging bits of shell, but don't dry the eggs. (A damp surface will help the smoke adhere to the egg whites.)

5. Place the eggs on the grate and smoke until the eggs take on a light brown patina from the smoke, about 25 minutes. Transfer the eggs to a cutting board, handling them as little as possible.

6. Slice each egg in half lengthwise with a sharp knife. Wipe any yolk off the blade before slicing the next egg. Gently remove the yolks and place them in a food processor. Pulse to break up the yolks. Add the mayo, mustard, paprika, and hot sauce. Season with salt and pepper to taste. Pulse until the filling is smooth. Add additional mayo 1 teaspoon at a time if the mixture is a little dry. (It shouldn't be too loose either.)

7.   Spoon the filling into each egg half or pipe it in using a small resealable plastic bag. You can also use a pastry bag fitted with a fluted tip.

8.   Place the eggs on a platter and lightly dust with paprika. Accompany with one or more of the suggested garnishes.

Roasted Red Pepper Dip

Servings: 8   Cooking Time: 45 Minutes

Ingredients:

- 4 red bell peppers, halved, destemmed, and deseeded
- 1 cup English walnuts, divided
- 1 small white onion, peeled and coarsely chopped
- 2 garlic cloves, peeled and smashed with a chef's knife
- ¼ cup extra virgin olive oil, plus more
- 1 tbsp balsamic vinegar or balsamic glaze
- 1 tsp honey (eliminate if using balsamic glaze)
- 1 tsp coarse salt, plus more
- 1 tsp ground cumin
- 1 tsp smoked paprika
- ½ to 1 tsp Aleppo red pepper flakes, plus more
- ¼ cup fresh white breadcrumbs (optional)
- distilled water (optional)
- assorted crudités or wedges of pita bread

Directions:

1.   Supply your smoker with wood pellets and follow the start-up procedure. Preheat the grill, with the lid closed, to 400° F.

2.   Place the peppers skin side down on the grate and grill until the skins blister and the flesh softens, about 30 minutes. Transfer the peppers to a bowl and cover with plastic wrap. Let cool to room temperature. Remove the skins with a paring knife or your fingers. Coarsely chop or tear the peppers.

3.   Place ¾ cup of walnuts in an aluminum foil roasting pan. Place the pan on the grate and toast for 10 to 15 minutes, stirring twice. Remove the pan from the grill and let the walnuts cool.

4.   Place the peppers, onion, garlic, and walnuts in a food processor fitted with the chopping blade. Pulse several times. Add the olive oil, balsamic vinegar, honey, salt, cumin, paprika, and red pepper flakes. Process until the mixture is fairly smooth. Taste for seasoning, adding more salt or red pepper flakes (if desired). (If the mixture is too loose, add breadcrumbs until the texture is to your liking. If it's too thick, add olive oil or water 1 tablespoon at a time.)

5.   Transfer the dip to a serving bowl. Use the back of a spoon to make a shallow depression in the center. Top with the remaining ¼ cup of walnuts and drizzle olive oil in the depression. Serve with crudités or pita bread.

Smoked Cheese

Servings: 4

Cooking Time: 150 Minutes

Ingredients:

➢   1 (2-pound) block medium Cheddar cheese, or your favorite cheese, quartered lengthwise

Directions:

1. Supply your smoker with wood pellets and follow the start-up procedure. Preheat the grill, with the lid closed, to 90°F.

2. Place the cheese directly on the grill grate and smoke for 2 hours, 30 minutes, checking frequently to be sure it's not melting. If the cheese begins to melt, try flipping it. If that doesn't help, remove it from the grill and refrigerate for about 1 hour and then return it to the cold smoker.

3. Remove the cheese, place it in a zip-top bag, and refrigerate overnight.

4. Slice the cheese and serve with crackers, or grate it and use for making a smoked mac and cheese.

Simple Cream Cheese Sausage Balls

Servings: 5

Cooking Time: 30 Minutes

Ingredients:

- 1 pound ground hot sausage, uncooked
- 8 ounces cream cheese, softened
- 1 package mini filo dough shells

Directions:

1. Supply your smoker with wood pellets and follow the start-up procedure. Preheat, with the lid closed, to 350°F.

2. In a large bowl, using your hands, thoroughly mix together the sausage and cream cheese until well blended.

3. Place the filo dough shells on a rimmed perforated pizza pan or into a mini muffin tin.

4. Roll the sausage and cheese mixture into 1-inch balls and place into the filo shells.

5. Place the pizza pan or mini muffin tin on the grill, close the lid, and smoke the sausage balls for 30 minutes, or until cooked through and the sausage is no longer pink.

6. Plate and serve warm.

COCKTAILS RECIPES

Grilled Peach Sour Cocktail

Servings: 2

Cooking Time: 15 Minutes

Ingredients:

- 2 peach, sliced
- 2 Tablespoon sugar
- 1 1/2 Ounce Smoked Simple Syrup
- 4 Ounce bourbon
- 6 Dash Bitters Lab Apricot Vanilla Bitters
- 2 Sprig fresh thyme, for garnish

Directions:

1. Supply your smoker with wood pellets and follow the start-up procedure. Preheat the grill, with the lid closed, to 325° F.

2. Toss peach slices with granulated sugar and place directly on grill grate. Cook for 20 minutes or until grill marks form. Remove from grill and let cool. Grill: 325 ℉

3. Place peaches and Traeger Smoked Simple Syrup into tin and muddle. Peaches should form about an ounce of juice during the muddling. Once completed, add remaining ingredients and shake.

4. Pour contents into glass over fresh ice and garnish with fresh thyme. Enjoy!

Smoked Plum And Thyme Fizz Cocktail

Servings: 2

Cooking Time: 60 Minutes

Ingredients:

➢ 6 fresh plums

➢ 4 Fluid Ounce vodka

➢ 1 1/2 Fluid Ounce fresh lemon juice

➢ 2 Ounce smoked plum and thyme simple syrup

➢ 4 Fluid Ounce club soda

➢ 2 Slices smoked plum, for garnish

➢ 2 Sprig fresh thyme, for garnish

➢ 8 Sprig thyme

➢ 2 Cup Smoked Simple Syrup

Directions:

1. Supply your smoker with wood pellets and follow the start-up procedure. Preheat the grill, with the lid closed, to 180° F.

2. Cut plums in half and remove the pit. Place the plum halves directly on the grill grate and smoke for 25 minutes. Grill: 180 °F

3. For the Plum and Thyme Simple Syrup: After 25 minutes, remove plums from the grill and cut into quarters. Add plums and thyme sprigs to 1 cup of Traeger Smoked Simple Syrup. Smoke the mixture for 45 minutes. Remove from grill, strain and let cool. Grill: 180 °F

4. Add vodka, fresh lemon juice and smoked plum and thyme simple syrup to a mixing glass.

5. Add ice and shake. Strain over clean ice, top off with club soda and garnish with a piece of thyme and slice of smoked plum. Enjoy!

Traeger Old Fashioned

Servings: 2

Cooking Time: 60 Minutes

Ingredients:

- ➢ 2 orange
- ➢ 2 Cup cherries
- ➢ 3 Ounce bourbon
- ➢ 1 Ounce Smoked Simple Syrup
- ➢ 8 Dash Bitters Lab Apricot Vanilla Bitters

Directions:

1. Supply your smoker with wood pellets and follow the start-up procedure. Preheat the grill, with the lid closed, to 180° F.

2. While Traeger preheats, slice whole orange into wheels.

3. Place cherries on a small sheet pan and place in the Traeger. Place orange slices directly on the grill grate.

4. Smoke cherries for 1 hour and oranges for 25 minutes, depending on taste, before removing from the grill. Let oranges and cherries cool. Grill: 180 °F

5. Pour bourbon into glass, followed by Traeger Smoked Simple Syrup and bitters. Add ice and stir for 45 seconds or until drink is well-diluted.

6. Strain contents into new glass over fresh ice. Skewer orange wheel and add cherry for garnish. Enjoy!

Traeger Paloma Cocktail

Servings: 2

Cooking Time: 25 Minutes

Ingredients:

- 4 grapefruit, halved
- Smoked Simple Syrup
- 10 Stick cinnamon
- 3 Ounce reposado tequila
- 1 Ounce lime juice
- 1 Ounce Smoked Simple Syrup
- grilled lime, for garnish
- cinnamon stick, for garnish

Directions:

1. Supply your smoker with wood pellets and follow the start-up procedure. Preheat the grill, with the lid closed, to 350° F.

2. Grilled Grapefruit Juice: Cut 2 grapefruits in half. Place a cinnamon stick in each grapefruit half and glaze with Traeger Smoked Simple Syrup. Place on grill grate and cook for 20 minutes or until edges start to burn and it acquires grill marks. Remove from heat and let cool. Grill: 350 °F

3. After grapefruits have cooled, squeeze and strain juice. It should yield 10 to 12 ounces of juice.

4. In a mixing glass, add tequila, lime juice, Traeger Smoked Simple Syrup and 2 ounces of the grilled grapefruit juice.

5. Add ice and shake. Strain over ice in an old fashioned glass.

6. Add a grilled lime slice and cinnamon stick to garnish. Enjoy!

Smoked Ice Mojito Slurpee

Servings: 2

Cooking Time: 30 Minutes

Ingredients:

- water
- 1 Cup white rum
- 1/2 Cup lime juice
- 1/4 Cup Smoked Simple Syrup
- 12 Whole fresh mint leaves
- 4 Sprig mint
- 4 Whole lime wedge, for garnish

Directions:

1. Supply your smoker with wood pellets and follow the start-up procedure. Preheat the grill, with the lid closed, to 180° F.
2. For optimal flavor, use Super Smoke if available. Grill: 180 °F
3. Remove water from grill and pour smoked water into ice cube trays. Place in freezer until frozen.
4. Add rum, lime juice, Traeger Smoked Simple Syrup, mint and smoked ice to a blender.
5. Blend until a slushy consistency and pour into glasses.
6. Garnish with a mint sprig and lime wedge. Enjoy!

Smoked Eggnog

Servings: 4

Cooking Time: 60 Minutes

Ingredients:

- 2 Cup whole milk
- 1 Cup heavy cream
- 4 egg yolk
- Cup sugar
- 3 Ounce bourbon
- 1 Teaspoon vanilla extract
- 1 Teaspoon nutmeg
- 4 egg white
- whipped cream

Directions:

1. Plan ahead, this recipe requires chill time.

2. Supply your smoker with wood pellets and follow the start-up procedure. Preheat the grill, with the lid closed, to 180° F.

3. Pour the milk and the cream into a baking pan and smoke on the Traeger for 60 minutes. Grill: 180 °F

4. Meanwhile, in the bowl of a stand mixer, beat the egg yolks until they lighten in color. Gradually add 1/3 cup sugar and continue to beat until sugar completely dissolves.

5. After the milk and cream have smoked, add them along with the bourbon, vanilla and nutmeg into the egg mixture and stir to combine.

6. Place the egg whites in the bowl of a stand mixer and beat to soft peaks. When you lift the beaters the whites will make a peak that slightly curls down.

7. With the mixer still running, gradually add 1 tablespoon of sugar and beat until stiff peaks form.

8. Gently fold the egg whites into the cream mixture and then whisk to thoroughly combine.

9. Chill eggnog for a couple hours to let the flavors meld. Garnish with a dash of nutmeg and whipped cream on top. Enjoy!

Honey Glazed Grapefruit Shandy Cocktail

Servings: 2

Cooking Time: 20 Minutes

Ingredients:

- 4 grapefruits
- 4 Tablespoon honey
- granulated sugar
- 2 Ounce bourbon
- 1 Ounce Smoked Simple Syrup
- 4 Ounce honey glazed grilled grapefruit, juiced
- 2 Bottle Ballast Point Grapefruit Sculpin

Directions:

1. Supply your smoker with wood pellets and follow the start-up procedure. Preheat the grill, with the lid closed, to 375° F.

2. For the honey glazed grapefruit: Slice one grapefruit in half and coat with 2 tablespoons honey.

3. Take the other grapefruit and slice into wheels. Toss the wheels in granulated sugar until well coated.

4. Place the grapefruit halves and wheels directly on the grill grate, cut side down, and cook for 20 to 30 minutes. Remove from grill and set the wheels aside. Grill: 375 ˚F

5. Squeeze the grapefruit halves into a measuring cup. It should yield about 2 oz juice.

6. Pour the grapefruit juice into a shaker and add bourbon and Traeger Smoked Simple Syrup then top with ice. Shake for 10-15 seconds.

7. Strain into glass, add ice and fill with beer. Garnish with the grilled grapefruit wheel. Enjoy!

Fig Slider Cocktail

Servings: 2

Cooking Time: 15 Minutes

Ingredients:

- 2 peach, halved
- 4 oranges
- honey
- sugar
- 2 Teaspoon orange fig spread
- 1 Ounce fresh lemon juice
- 4 Ounce bourbon
- 3 Ounce honey glazed grilled orange juice

Directions:

1. Supply your smoker with wood pellets and follow the start-up procedure. Preheat the grill, with the lid closed, to 325° F.

2. Pit the peach and cut in half. Cut one of the oranges in half. Glaze the peach and orange cut sides with honey and set directly on the grill grate until the honey caramelizes and fruit has grill marks. Grill: 325 ˚F

3. Cut the second orange into wheels and coat with granulated sugar on both sides. Place directly on the grill grate and cook 15 minutes each side or until grill marks form. Grill: 325 ˚F

4. In a mixing tin, add grilled peaches, bourbon, orange fig spread, fresh lemon juice and honey glazed orange juice.

5. Shake vigorously to blend the juices and fig spread. Strain over clean ice. Garnish with grilled orange wheel. Enjoy!

Grilled Blood Orange Mimosa

Servings: 4

Cooking Time: 15 Minutes

Ingredients:

- ➢ 3 blood orange, halved
- ➢ 2 Tablespoon granulated sugar
- ➢ 1 Bottle sparkling wine
- ➢ thyme sprigs, for garnish

Directions:

1. Supply your smoker with wood pellets and follow the start-up procedure. Preheat the grill, with the lid closed, to 375° F.

2. When the grill is hot, dip the cut side of the orange halves in sugar and place cut side down directly on the grill grate. Grill: 375 ℉

3. Grill the oranges for 10-15 minutes or until grill marks develop. Grill: 375 ℉

4. Remove from the grill and let cool at room temperature.

5. When cool enough to handle, juice the oranges and strain through a fine strainer removing any pulp.

6. Pour 5 oz of sparkling wine into each glass and top with 1 oz blood orange juice.

7. Garnish with a sprig of thyme. Enjoy!

Grilled Peach Mint Julep

Servings: *2*

Cooking Time: 45 Minutes

Ingredients:

- 2 Whole peach
- 4 Ounce whiskey
- 2 Cup sugar
- 4 Tablespoon pink peppercorns
- 20 Whole fresh mint leaves, plus more for garnish
- 2 lime wedge, for garnish
- 4 Ounce bourbon

Directions:

1. For the Grilled Whiskey Peaches: cut peach into slices, then soak peach slices in whiskey in the refrigerator for 4 to 6 hours.

2. For the Pink Peppercorn Simple Syrup: In a shallow pan, combine sugar, 1 cup water and pink peppercorns.

3. Supply your smoker with wood pellets and follow the start-up procedure. Preheat the grill, with the lid closed, to 180° F.

4. Cook syrup down on the grill for 30 minutes, or until desired smoke flavor has been reached. Remove from the grill. Grill: 180 °F

5. Increase Traeger temperature to 350°F and preheat. Place the whiskey peach slices directly on the grill grate and cook 10 to 12 minutes or until peaches soften and get grill marks. Grill: 350 °F

6. To make the Julep: Muddle 1/2 ounce Pink Peppercorn Simple Syrup with 10 fresh mint leaves and 4 slices of grilled whiskey peaches.

7. Add crushed ice over the rim of the glass. Pour bourbon over the crushed ice and stir. Garnish with 1 large sprig of mint and fresh lime. Enjoy!